A TASTE OF HEAVEN

*A Biblical glimpse
at the glories to come*

Larry R. Dick

Printed in Victoria, Canada

National Library of Canada Cataloguing in Publication Data

Dick, Larry R., 1944-
    A taste of Heaven : a biblical glimpse at the glories
to come / Larry R. Dick.
ISBN 1-55369-726-X
    I. Title.
BT846.3.D52 2002   236'.24   C2002-903251-2

TRAFFORD

This book was published *on-demand* **in cooperation with Trafford Publishing.**
On-demand publishing is a unique process and service of making a book available for retail sale to the public taking advantage of on-demand manufacturing and Internet marketing. **On-demand publishing** includes promotions, retail sales, manufacturing, order fulfilment, accounting and collecting royalties on behalf of the author.

Suite 6E, 2333 Government St., Victoria, B.C. V8T 4P4, CANADA

Phone	250-383-6864	Toll-free	1-888-232-4444 (Canada & US)
Fax	250-383-6804	E-mail	sales@trafford.com
Web site	www.trafford.com	TRAFFORD PUBLISHING IS A DIVISION OF TRAFFORD HOLDINGS LTD.
Trafford Catalogue #02-0539		www.trafford.com/robots/02-0539.html	

10   9   8   7   6   5   4   3   2

TABLE OF CONTENTS

ACKNOWLEDGMENTS

Every author is helped by an army of supporters and encouragers. I would like to mention a few of these special people. Thanks first to my wife Gayle, for her undying enthusiasm and helpful editing comments, then to our dear friend Ruth Moyle, to Dr. Dell Johnson and the faculty of Pensacola Theological Seminary, and to my father-in-law Walter Prescott, who gave me the idea in the first place and to whom this book is dedicated, and who is now enjoying all the glories of heaven firsthand.

INTRODUCTION

Is heaven your final answer?

You may never sit in the hot seat of TV's "Who wants to be a Millionaire?" But believe me, how you answer the question of heaven will be worth far more than one million dollars. But how can you answer what you know so little about? I hope this book will fill in some of those blanks for you. Most of all I pray it will lead you to trust the lifeline of God's Word and give you a taste of heaven.

"What do you mean, 'you don't know if you will like Heaven,' I thought you were looking forward to it?"

"I am, I just don't know very much about it and I really like what God's given us here on earth . . . this I can enjoy."

Looking around I had to agree with his last statement. The sun shimmered and sparkled across the ruffled waters of the sound and pine trees etched a dark green outline against the perfect blue of another cloudless Florida day. Graceful sails glided silently towards the horizon. An enticing scent of barbecue hung in the air, and squeals of childish laughter drifted down the narrow beach.

We sat on stone picnic benches and watched power-boats, sail boats, catamarans, pontoons, jet-skis and even a commercial fishing craft being launched and recovered from the town's new boat ramp. Across the sound we could see the hotels and high-rises of the outer beaches outlined with a soft white haze rising from the pure silica sand of the Emerald Coast's beautiful shores.

Surely this was already paradise and a taste of heaven?

"It isn't I'm not ready to go to heaven. It just doesn't seem very real to me. The Bible tells us so little about what heaven is like. I find it hard to look forward to."

This was my father-in-law speaking, a man whose quiet, godly wisdom I had so admired since I first dated his daughter. This was the man with whom I had enjoyed hours of discussing the word of God and the problems of life. If he wasn't sure what heaven was like then probably few people were.

So began a journey of asking others what they knew of heaven, of examining my own limited knowledge of heaven in the Scriptures, giving me a dissertation topic for my PhD. Does the Bible tell us specifically what heaven will be like? What will the new earth and the capital city, New Jerusalem, be like?

Is it a real, physical place or just some kind of spiritual realm unlike anything on earth? What will people look like in heaven? What will we do forever and ever? Will there be buildings, families, nations in heaven? What language will we speak? Where is heaven? Will we see God there?

This book is based on my doctoral research. However, it is not written as a systematic theology of heaven but simply to present a Biblical picture of what eternity will be like.

My hope is to bring new excitement and understanding to the average person in the pew, as well as to the Bible scholar. Perhaps it will even encourage those who do not believe everything in the Bible but do believe in a heaven.

Yes, I believe the Bible tells us much about what Heaven will be like. Eden, the tabernacle, the promised land, the kingdom parables, the millennial kingdom, New Jerusalem, all paint a picture of eternity. Many of the great themes and teachings of Scripture present, at the very least, a type or taste of what Heaven will be like.

"Eye hath not seen, nor ear heard, neither have entered into the heart of man, the things which God hath prepared for them that love him. But God hath revealed them unto us by his Spirit" (1 Cor. 2:9,10).

I pray the Biblical picture presented here will make heaven a much more tangible, real place to you. May it bring new hope and understanding of heaven's glories to everyone who reads it, especially to the bereaved, the lonely, the hurting and the discouraged. May it bless your heart.

Life is short and so full of troubles. The good things of this world are so temporary. They are but a taste of better, eternal things to come. Only those things which last forever are real and worthwhile.

"In thy presence is fullness of joy; at thy right hand are pleasures forevermore" (Psa. 16:11).

PART I.

A NEW HOPE

CHAPTER 1

WHERE IN THE WORLD IS HEAVEN ?

What If I Don't Like Cities?

People running, people screaming, sirens howling, there was chaos all over the TV screen! Standing inside the CNN Center in Atlanta watching a re-run of the 1996 Olympic bombing I felt glad I no longer lived in a city. Traffic gridlock near the airport, warning signs about muggers and pick-pockets in the Underground Market, and less than spotless downtown streets and sidewalks, only added to the feeling. Atlanta is a terrific city. It's people who spoil it. The rain didn't help either.

If heaven's a city I'm not so sure I want to spend forever there.

The next morning changed my perspective. I pulled back the drapes of my seventeenth floor Buckhead hotel room and gazed out of the huge bay window at a cloudless blue sky above a rolling carpet of dark green. I never realized Atlanta had so many trees. Away to the south, in the center of my vision, a bright and beautiful city hovered between tree and sky. Its tall buildings shimmered, white and spotless in the early morning sunlight.

Then it hit me. What if this city really was spotlessly clean? What if it was a city where there was no fear of getting mugged, ripped off, or blown apart, a city where you could never be lost or even ignored? Imagine a city where everyone was kind and helpful, happy, honest, morally pure, and a relative!

There is such a city, New Jerusalem, where everyone will be recognized, loved and accepted. Surely the heavenly city is a city no one would ever want to leave. It is a city already prepared for

3

the redeemed (Rev. 21:2). I don't know about you, but I could get used to living in a city like that.

But there's much more to heaven than just a city, as you'll discover in the following chapters. It's not just the last chapters of Revelation which show us what heaven is like. The Bible is packed throughout with glimpses of eternity. So what is this place called heaven?

Cruising the island-dotted waters of the Caribbean, being waited on hand and foot, dining daily before sumptuous spreads, this is my idea of heaven. At least one of them! Spending time with family, laughing with my kids, walking the beach with my wife at sunset, enjoying the peace of God in the early morning privacy of our own backyard. These are a taste of heaven to me.

So what is heaven to you? Is it a vacation in Hawaii, a high mountain trail, a seat at the Super-bowl, golfing at St. Andrews, the deck of a cruise ship, or anywhere free from bosses, in-laws, outlaws and the IRS? We all have different ideas and dreams of heaven. They vary from culture to culture and age to age.

Sensual pleasure and personal luxuries are looked forward to in the Muslim view of heaven. Hindus expect a heaven of flowers, music, laughter and happiness on the banks of a river. Buddhists look for a paradise reached only after a series of reincarnations and self improvement. The Greeks and Egyptians hoped for the reward of immortality and blissful existence of the soul. The American Indian longed for an eternal happy hunting ground gained through bravery in the crucible of war.

Even the communists embalm their dead heroes in the apparent hope of reaching a classless utopia beyond the grave. The common thread in all of this is the desire for immortality, material and spiritual reward, and the hope of a better life to come. So let's try and define this common hope called heaven.

How Do You Define Heaven?
God's abode or dwelling place is how the dictionary defines it. *The final place the blessed go to after death* is a secondary explanation. Heaven is also the sky, the blue expanse that surrounds the earth, and the place of the sun, moon and stars.

Heaven is further defined as a state, as well as a place, namely a state of supreme bliss or happiness. Some dictionaries even generalize heaven as being any place of happiness or contentment. Heaven is also defined as deity itself, a synonym for God.

Paradise, kingdom, temple, home, are some of the Biblical words used to describe heaven. Paradise (meaning *garden*), was man's first home. The kingdom (of heaven) is the believer's final home. God's throne is in Heaven. It is His home. In eternity His home becomes the believer's home and God dwells there forever with man.

In the beginning man's home included the earth and the whole universe (Gen.1:1). So in eternity man's home will include a new earth and universe. The word *heaven* in the Scriptures can refer to three different things; the atmosphere, space, and the heaven of heavens (where God and the angels live). This heaven of heavens is the same as the Apostle Paul's third heaven (2 Cor. 12:2), where he was given a glimpse of paradise.

Thus the sky is the first heaven and the stellar regions or space constitute the second heaven, and the throne room of God is the third heaven. There is some indication that within the second heaven is the spiritual realm around the earth. This is the dimension where Satan and his demons do battle with the angels of God over the affairs of men on earth, the *high places* of Ephesians 6:12.

What Are the Bible Words for Heaven?

Shamayim is the predominant Hebrew word translated as heaven in the Old Testament. Its root meaning is high or elevated. Throughout the Bible God is always on high, and heaven is always above the earth. It is found 397 times (KJV) along with its other form of *shamayin* (38 times).

The most frequent use of the word *heaven* in the Bible is in the phrase *God of heaven* or *God in heaven*. So ultimately heaven is where God is. But God is everywhere isn't he? Of course, and when Solomon dedicated the first temple in Jerusalem he acknowledged that no temple nor even the heaven of heavens could contain God (1Kgs.8).

5

God temporarily chose to show his presence and glory in a particular place on earth (the temple). He has permanently chosen to rule the earth and affairs of men from a particular place called heaven. This is God's primary dwelling place (Psa.11:14).

Ouranos is the Greek word translated as heaven in the New Testament. It comes from a root word *oro* meaning to rise. This word *oro* is also used for mountain or hill. Like *shamayim* it has two basic meanings, referring either to the universe or to the abode of God.

These Old and New Testament words for heaven are found 738 times in 700 different verses in the Bible (KJV). Approximately 311 of these occurrences refer specifically to eternity, the third heaven, the abode of God. Why am I explaining all this? To show heaven is an incredible, complex, wonderful place and the Bible gives us much more detail about it than perhaps you realized.

Mankind was created by God to have fellowship with him. Nothing else has ever been created in God's image like man. Sin destroyed this relationship. The cross of Christ restores it for all those who believe. Thus man's final state in eternity is to live in fellowship with God again forever. This final, eternal state and place of the redeemed is what this book is all about.

Heaven in this book refers to the new earth and universe, the city of God, New Jerusalem. This includes the throne room of God. It does not refer to the millennium (one thousand-year rule of Christ on this earth), nor to the intermediate state, though we will talk about these things later. When we speak of heaven we mean both the physical and spiritual existence of the redeemed, living with God forever and ever.

Can I Really Know What Heaven Is Like?

Specific information on what heaven will be like is hard to find. Little has been written about it in recent years. Three times as many books written in the nineteenth century had heaven in their titles as those written in the twentieth century. In Christian magazines and theological journals much more emphasis has been given to healings, happiness, heresies and hell than to heaven! Even Systematic Theologies devote far more pages to hell than to heaven. That really surprised me. I would have thought heaven was just as important a doctrine as hell, which it is!

There are however, many excellent commentaries on the Book of Revelation that do examine many of the specific Biblical concepts of what heaven will be like. Actually, you will probably learn more from good eschatology (end times) books about heaven than anywhere else.

It seems from conversations with others, much of what people know about heaven comes from church hymnals. Many of the great hymns of the faith speak eloquently about the glories of heaven. Unfortunately it is usually couched in the vague spiritual language of the "sweet bye and bye," with visions of everyone floating on clouds playing a harp! While commendably maintaining the church's hope, they tell you little about what living in heaven will really be like.

But isn't this because heaven is just too wonderful to be understood? Wrong! How can you hope for something you don't have a clue about? This is why God has given you the Bible, and the Holy Spirit, so you can begin to understand now, the infinite purposes and promises of God (1 Cor. 2:9-10). Of course there are limitations to your present understanding of heaven. Nevertheless the Bible does give you a pretty good picture, or *taste* if you like, of the awesome future in store for all Christ's followers.

Jesus spoke much about heaven. The Old Testament saints had specific expectations of what heaven would be like (Heb. 11:10,13-16). There are numerous *types* of heaven throughout Scripture that give you, at the very least, a taste of heaven.

But heaven is eternal, infinite and on a spiritual plane, isn't it? So can you ever really know what it will be like? Does the Bible reveal physical and spiritual details for you? Much more than most people know! After all, someone actually came from heaven to show you. Jesus confirms the truth of God's revelation. No one else in history has ever claimed to have been there, much less be God himself in human form!

Jesus is unique. The Word is accurate. Every other religion claims to show you how to get to heaven. Jesus brings heaven to you. His Word not only tells you how to go there but reveals

7

everything you need to know to begin experiencing heaven now (Eph. 1:4; 2:5-6).

Besides Jesus, there are other eye-witness accounts of heaven in the Bible. Many Old and New Testament saints were given glimpses into heaven and heaven's throne room: Moses and the 70 elders (Exod. 24:10), Micaiah (1 Kgs. 22:19), Elisha and his servant (2 Kgs. 6:17), Isaiah (Isa. 6:1-5), Ezekiel (Ezek. 1:4-28), Daniel (Dan. 7-10), Stephen (Acts 7:49,55), Paul (2 Cor. 12:2), and John (Revelation), for example.

But heaven is not just an experience, it is a physical reality. As you explore with me the Biblical descriptions of heaven, I hope you'll gain a new excitement for this incredible, marvelous place.

Time-bound earthlings have difficulty understanding heaven and eternity. Forever is beyond our experience. If your senses can't discern it then you tend not to believe it. Or so you tell yourself. You can't see the wind or electricity yet you experience the effects of these things. Therefore you believe in them and use them, or at least develop a healthy respect for their power.

Similarly with spiritual and supernatural concepts, you often experience the effects of believing them before fully understanding them. You can't prove everything by intellect or sensual experience. Even if you could, you wouldn't have time! When was the last time you checked out the Power Company or the electrical circuit in your house *before* you flipped the light switch?

Whether you admit it or not, life is lived by constant acts of faith. It's not *if* you can live by faith but rather who or what you are prepared to put your faith in. The Bible is God's revelation to man, not man's ideas about God (Prov. 30:5; 2 Tim. 3:16). So you can, by faith, completely trust what it says about heaven.

Yes, your understanding of heaven is going to be limited because you are part of a fallen and finite race. You can never fully appreciate the glories of heaven before experiencing them. But Jesus has experienced heaven.

Is Heaven a Place or a State

Abraham longed for a heavenly city (Heb. 11: 10,16). He was also given covenant (irrevocable) promises of land (Gen. 13:14-

17). Jesus told his disciples there were many mansions (homes) in heaven (Jn. 14:2-3). Twice in this passage Jesus calls heaven a *place* and once a *house*.

Heaven is much more than just a state of spiritual bliss in the presence of God. It is a very real place. At Christ's ascension the disciples watched Jesus physically go through the clouds into heaven. They were told he would return in the same (physical) way (Acts 1:9-11).

Abraham was brought up in a great and wealthy city (Ur). Surely his hope was not just in some future state of heavenly well being but in a real live city. David believed his people Israel would one day rule over all the land God had promised them.

Many Bible scholars would claim these land, homes, and city promises will be fulfilled by the Jews in the millennial kingdom. Yet every one of these promises are forever. The thousand year rule of the millennium is just that, one thousand years! It is not forever. Thus I believe the millennium itself has to be a continuing type (or pattern) of what will be in heaven, the eternal kingdom.

Yes, heaven is a very real place, even a prepared place Jesus said (Jn. 14). It is much, much more that just a state of mind or spirit. So then where is this place?

Where Is Heaven Located?

Beyond the clouds, beyond the stars lies the city of God, heaven (Job 22:12; Isa. 14:13-14). Heaven is always above the earth (Psa. 102:19, 103:11). It is distant and hidden from earth. Wherever God's throne is, that is heaven (Psa. 103:19: Acts 7:49). His throne has been forever (Psa.93:2). This throne is part of God's temple in heaven (Psa. 11:4). This temple is synonymous with the city of God, also referred to as Zion and New Jerusalem.

The city is described as being on the sides of the north, in relation to earth (Psa. 48:2; Isa. 14:13). The Hebrew phrase here means angle or corner that points towards the north. In Solomon's day the temple site would have been in the northeast corner, the northern angle of the city of David.

So what does all this mean? It means heaven (at this point, the heavenly city) is a definite, physical place already built and prepared for the redeemed. It is currently located somewhere out there to the north beyond the stars.

Well if this is true, why can't you just go there now in a space shuttle? Limits of technology aside, heaven is also located on a spiritual plane, a fourth dimension or parallel universe, if you like. At present it is only accessed by humans through death or translation.

Angels are spirit beings who live in a spiritual realm. They also appear in the presence of God in His throne room in heaven. God (the Father) is spirit. Therefore heaven, while having physical aspects is also in a spiritual realm. Yet at the same time heaven is also within the believer, whose body is presently a temple of the Holy Spirit (1 Cor. 3:16).

As a result, heaven, at least for believers, is all around you right now (Eph. 2:6). Because it is another dimension, you can only see it if God permits or you are especially spiritually discerning like Elisha (2 Kgs. 6:17). But whether you see it or not, heaven is there!

Sounds kind of mind boggling, doesn't it? Our technological Western world finds it hard to acknowledge the reality of the spiritual realm. Third world countries and cultures are much more aware of these things.

Heaven's just not logical or scientific, your mind tells you. Yet since the advent of quantum physics and Einstein's theories of relativity, even the scientific community admits the possibility of other dimensions. They just don't know how to access them if they exist. The Bible declares heaven does exist. It is a present reality as well as a future hope.

Translation physically into heaven is recorded only a few times in the Bible. Enoch walked with God and was quietly taken into heaven (Gen. 5:24). Elijah went up in a tornado with chariots of fire (2 Kgs. 2:11). Jesus ascended through the clouds into heaven (Acts 1:9-11).

Everyone else in the Scriptures died first and then only their spirits entered heaven to await the resurrection. Jesus taught angels carry believers into heaven (Luke 16: 22). Isaiah, Daniel, Ezekiel, Paul, John were allowed to see into heaven, whether in body or in spirit the Bible is not clear, but each one remained on earth to die later.

One day all believers, living on earth when Jesus returns for His church, will be raptured (snatched up) physically into heaven. Thus the only way to access heaven is through death, special translation of God, or at the rapture. Each one of these requires personal faith in the Savior, Jesus Christ.

So what difference does a belief in heaven make? Why do we fear death and long for immortality? Why does our world seem so hopeless? We'll examine these and other related questions in the next chapter.

CHAPTER 2

WHY SHOULD I CARE ABOUT HEAVEN ?

Why Does Society Seem To Have So Little Hope?

Suicide was the last thing I expected from this young man. Yet there it was glaring at me from our local newspaper. Early in the morning he had driven alone into the woods and shot himself to death. Sure, his self-esteem had seemed a little low when I'd first met with him in the parsonage, but nothing beyond the normal fears of preparing to get married, worrying about money, and finishing school.

On the surface he seemed to have everything going for him. Like many today, this young man had previously sought for satisfaction in all the wrong places. While pursuing the party life at college he'd become immersed in "Dungeons & Dragons," and the occult. Then he met a sweet young Christian lady, fell in love and suddenly life felt good again. But the demons of his past apparently caught up with him.

What man feels and experiences with his senses is all there is to life. This is the prevailing philosophy of modern life. Live for the moment and don't even think about tomorrow, let alone eternity. There are no absolutes. Truth is relative (what is *is*?). We evolved from animals so why not live like one?

No wonder suicide is a leading killer of our young people. If death ends it all and there is no life after death, then what meaning or purpose is there to life, even when it's successful? If the best we hope for is a million in the bank we must all despair! Statistically most of us will never achieve this hope. Even for those who do, the reality is life is still a constant series of worries, trials and disappointments. So how does a belief in heaven change all that?

Image is everything, youth valued more than age, a focus on self, and avoidance of pain at all costs. This is the result of a society that has no belief in heaven. For many who say they do believe in heaven it is often just fire-insurance against the possibility of judgment and hell, and not a daily reality.

The accepted view is anyone who is too heavenly minded is no earthly use. In reality the opposite is true. Those who truly set their minds on heaven do the most earthly good. Why? Because a belief in heaven and the hope of future reward encourages believers to endure hardships on earth patiently and to live unselfish, Godly lives in service to others. The hope of heaven can also give meaning and purpose to the struggles of life, especially to those who suffer.

For man cannot live without hope. A belief in the reality of heaven is essential then to the present as well as the future well-being of man. Pain has no point or purpose to those without hope of heaven. So society produces Dr. Kevorkians to free us from such indignities. We say we fear the pain not the dying. But this is simply denial of our fear of the unknown.

Perhaps there is life after death. Maybe there is a judgment or even hell. You just can't get away from thoughts of eternity (Eccl. 3:11). All your life creation has shown you the beauty, order and holiness of God. You know you deserve judgment. You are without excuse (Rom. 1:18-20).

This is why you fear death. It is Satan's final weapon. So there is a natural revulsion to death even for the believer. But in Christ there really is no fear of death, only a glorious hope of heaven and a far, far better life to come.

Immortality, did you know, is the number one public desire? It is the ultimate achievement. Surveys have shown the longing for immortality comes even before power, love and money.[1] This

---

[1]Benjamin D. Saurez, 7 Steps to Freedom II (Canton, Ohio: Hanford Press, 1994), 2-31.

desire for immortality is seen in the growing interest in cryonics. The hope is science will advance enough one day to bring these frozen bodies back to life. The advances in genetic engineering has led to a similar desire for personal cloning.

Man instinctively knows there is more to life than this earthly existence (Rom. 1:19-20). Every culture has a belief in some kind of immortality. Not only the world's religions but its philosophy, literature, poetry, art, music and drama have given considerable attention to life after death. The universal hope is for a better life not just lack of dying. Nobody wants quantity without quality.

Yet these world views give little hope of anything more than a ghostly beyond. Only the Bible's heaven offers real, tangible hope for immortality. Resurrection, new bodies, a new and perfect universe, a glorious heavenly city, material wealth, physical and spiritual joy forever, now this is a heaven worth living for!

Why Is the Promise of Heaven So Important?

Hoping for something better in the future gives meaning and purpose to almost everything we do now. Athletes give up hours of their day to willingly punish their bodies in the hope of a gold medal, a Super-bowl ring, or a silver cup. Countless corporate employees sacrifice time, leisure activities and sometimes their families in the hope of future financial independence.

If we are so ready to sacrifice and work hard in the hope of temporary and uncertain future rewards, how much more should we be motivated to work for guaranteed eternal rewards? This is why the promise of heaven is so important.

The knowledge of what heaven offers you can increase your self-esteem, transform your priorities, make sense out of suffering, and bring hope and comfort in the face of death. You see, it doesn't matter if you never amount to much by the world's standards. If you have surrendered your life to Christ now, then you are already the child of a King. In heaven you will receive a princely inheritance beyond anything this world could ever offer you. It will be yours forever!

Commitment, compassion, loyalty, endurance are rarely witnessed in a society that honors charisma above character. Self-centeredness, instant gratification, worship of material things, all result from a lack of belief in the eternal.

The promise and hope of heaven changes all this. Heaven gives you a reason to live, and to resist all that is selfish and evil. Character, compassion, love and relationships now become more important to you than things.

History teaches you many of the greatest achievements and discoveries came from those with a firm view of heaven and eternity, from Galileo to the Founding Fathers of America. The universe itself declares the vastness, beauty and order of God. It screams at you there is a heaven (Psa.19:1-4). From Genesis to Revelation the Bible refers constantly to heaven.

Many of the greatest names in science and the arts were Bible believers. Because of their belief of reward in heaven they were willing to sacrifice their lives in doing what would glorify God on earth. Thousands of believers throughout history have willingly died for their belief in the Prince of Heaven. Why would they do these things if heaven was just something they had made up? Why would the disciples and the other eye-witnesses of Jesus' resurrection willingly do the same if they knew it was a lie? There is a hope of glory. There is life after death. The Bible record is true.

The more you examine and learn of the universe you live in the more you are made aware of eternity. Nothing makes sense if this short life on earth is all there is. Go gaze at the stars and tell me it all just happened, that there is no creator God with whom you have to deal, that there is no heaven to hope for (Psa. 19:1-4)!

The Bible is very clear. The only life forms out there are God and the angels. The only destiny for man after death is heaven (where God is) or hell (eternal separation from God). Our minds, our wills, our emotions (our very souls) instinctively tell us we are much more than just animals in this universe. There is life after death. The question is, where will you spend it?

Nature's endless cycles demonstrate the fact of resurrection; summer (life), fall (dying), winter (death) and spring (new life). There is (physical) life after death even here. The fact that Jesus rose from the dead assures you of a real, physical heaven. Even his enemies could not disprove His resurrection. The best they could do was to spread lies and rumors (Matt. 28:11-15).

Two thousand year old seeds from the tombs of Egypt have been successfully grown to life again. The animal food chain demonstrates the endless cycle of death and rebirth within creation. Metamorphosis and the insect cycle of life is another example. Of course, all of nature has been affected by man's sin. So it currently presents an imperfect picture of resurrection and eternity.

Yet don't you just love spring? When I see the azaleas blooming all over our neighborhood and the grass has turned suddenly from brown to green I know summer's on its way and I'm glad to be alive. After a long winter the spring reminds you there is always the hope of new life ahead and better things to come. In Christ all things become new! For as in Adam all die, even so in Christ shall all be made alive (1 Cor. 15:22).

What Is the Significance of Heaven to the Church?

Earthly existence for the believer is meant to prepare you for heaven, Jesus taught (Matt. 6:20,33). Belonging to a local body of believers (a church), teaches you to experience heaven now. True worship and genuine Christian fellowship can only be experienced by those whose hearts are set on heaven. Desire for eternal rewards can motivate you to unselfish, compassionate love and service through the church.

The Scriptures urge the church to set its affections on things above (Col. 3:2). Without a sure hope in heaven and the resurrection the very gospel message of the church becomes meaningless (1 Cor. 15). Heaven lifts your eyes off of your own daily struggles and frees you to see and meet the needs of others. Genuine concern that friends, neighbors and loved ones might miss heaven and spend forever in hell gives great impetus to the spreading of the gospel.

The promise of heaven as a real home for eternity has sustained Old Testament patriarch, New Testament saint, and the church down through the ages. The promise and hope of heaven has been preserved and promoted through the hymns of the church, as well as through its teachings.

Ecological restoration of the earth and perfect government in the millennial kingdom will be a foretaste of heaven and eternity. The one thousand year rule of Christ on this present earth (Rev. 20:4-6) will fulfill the land and throne promises given to the Jews. These everlasting promises will continue for true Israel (all the people of God) in the new heaven and earth in eternity.

The millennium will be the only true "heaven on earth" prior to eternity. There will be perfect peace, perfect environment, perfect harmony within nature. The animals will be no longer kill or be killed (Isa. 65:25).

The only death for humans, during the millennium, will come from disobedience to Christ's rule from Jerusalem. Despite this perfect environment mankind will rebel against Jesus and the Jewish rule at the end of this one thousand years when Satan is let loose again on the earth. Then many nations will converge on Jerusalem to try and destroy the Prince of Peace, Jesus!

That's when God intervenes in judgment, destroying the earth and its systems with fire (2 Pet. 3:7-13). Then God reforms a new earth and universe, the final heaven of eternity. Thus the millennial kingdom is not heaven. But it is a type of heaven, the closest type in Scripture to the real thing. Why? Because Christ will be ruling as King together with his saints, just as He will in eternity.

Yes, there will be peace on earth, this earth. There will be a one-world perfect government for a thousand years. The destruction and pollution of this world will be cleaned up. The world will become similar to what it was like in Adam's day. But the millennium is not the eternal heaven. It is just an introduction, a foretaste of what's to come.

Just think about it for a moment. God in His mercy will give his saints another opportunity to come back and live in this old world we know and love so much. In our already glorified bodies we will be able to enjoy everything and every place we missed before only this time in a perfect and peaceful environment for a thousand years.

Wow! Isn't God good? But all of this seems so far off. What difference does heaven make to my life now?

What Is the Importance of Heaven Now?

Aging doesn't seem such a big deal anymore in the light of heaven. Material possessions are seen for what they really are, temporary entrustments. Heaven even begins to answer the *why's* of our lives. Death and dying, pain and suffering, abuse and neglect can be faced with new hope and purpose, no matter how unfair they seem.

Through prayer and faith you can experience heaven's peace now (Phil. 4:6-7). All of heaven's power is available to the believer in Jesus Christ, today. Heaven's angels are here, all around you, you just can't see them physically. You can face anything and anyone, today, because of heaven. What does it matter if they take your job, your possessions, your home, even your loved ones, or your life!

If you're killed it will only accelerate your way to heaven, and you'll see your loved ones again, forever. As for material losses, they will be more than replaced in heaven. Sounds a little crass and unfeeling? Yes it is, if heaven is not real. But it is!

Excitement about heaven was very evident in the early church. The Bible tells us many of the churches Paul established on his missionary travels thought Jesus was coming back in their lifetime. They were looking forward to the completion of their salvation. Paul, himself, who had the privilege of being given a glimpse into heaven, was so focused about going to be there with His Lord that he wrote, "for me to live is Christ and to die is gain" (Phil. 1:21).

How many of us could say this and really mean it. Most of us, if we are honest, would love to go to heaven . . . just not right now! Yet the Bible teaches heaven is your true home. Where your treasure is there is your heart. So seek first the things of heaven and everything else will take care of itself (Matt. 6:33).

In parable after parable Jesus taught about the kingdom of heaven, of the blessings and rewards waiting there for faithful believers. He did so to help His disciples understand what heaven would be like (Matt. 13:11). Paul declares in Ephesians that in Christ we already enjoy spiritual blessings from heaven. The fellowship of the church, for the saved person, is a spiritual example now of what heaven is like (Eph. 2:6).

From the beginning the Bible teaches the Sabbath day was given to remind you of heaven (Heb. 4:9-10). We'll explore this principle in more detail later. A focus on heaven now, and excitement for the Lord's return is given a special reward (2 Tim. 4:8). Heaven helps you forget the past and keep on going in the walk of faith (Ph. 3:13-14).

What Influence Does Heaven Have on Earth?

Political history is ruled by heaven. Though Satan is temporarily in control of the governments of the world, nothing happens to the nations without heaven's say so. Example after example occurs in the Old Testament of Heaven's control of empires. Deborah's song of victory over Sisera and his armies in Judges 5 tells us that every campaign on earth has its counterpart in the heavenlies. The angels and demons battle along with the armies on earth and directly influence the result.

God is sovereign and he rules the world from heaven. Pharaoh, Saul, David, Nebuchadnezzar, Cyrus, Darius, Herod, Pilate and the rulers of Canaan discovered first hand all their power was owed to Jehovah God.

Daniel's visions of empires past and future demonstrate very clearly that heaven plans and controls history. Significantly the book of Daniel highlights what the rest of Scripture teaches. All of earth's history centers on the person of Jesus Christ. Everything that happens to you will be a direct result of your response to this central figure of history, Christ. Ultimately it all comes down to this, for every country, ruler, and individual.

He, Jesus, is the only one who makes sense of history and our world. He has already influenced history, cultures, religion, literature, music and the arts, more than any other person. There will only be peace on earth when He returns from heaven. God has too much invested in us to let us totally destroy ourselves. There will only be perfect world government when He is on the throne in Jerusalem. But for now, Jesus' physical presence is in heaven. So who else is there?

Angels fill heaven's throne room. God the Father is there along with the Son and the Holy Spirit, ruling the world from on high.

Believers from throughout history are there. Old and New Testament saints are there, since the resurrection of Jesus (Rev. 7:9-12).

The missionaries, the ministers, the martyrs of the past, and all your loved ones who died in Christ are there. They are presently similar to the angels having a spiritual form. Unlike the angels they are awaiting the rapture when their spirits will reunite with their old bodies to be transformed instantly into glorious new ones (1 Cor. 15:52;1 Thess. 4:16-17).

The cherubim and seraphim are there. These are special angels and creatures of God that worship and serve Him day and night in His throne room. Heaven is already filled with countless believers, joyfully serving and worshipping the Lord together and looking for the end of the age. Together with the angels they celebrate each time a new person on earth becomes part of heaven's family through faith in Christ (Luke 15:7,10).

Jesus said he was going to prepare a place for you in the heavenly city. This is parallel to the Jewish wedding custom where the groom goes to his father's house after the betrothal to build a new separate, home for his bride and returns on the wedding night (Matt. 25:1-130).

Christ in his love and wisdom knows exactly the kind of home you would love to have in heaven. Maybe, just maybe, your loved ones who have gone on before you are assisting Christ in preparing your special place? Imagine if they were choosing the colors and the landscaping of your mansion right now?

Of course, God may have already completed each individual home in New Jerusalem. We do know the city itself is already built. But it is an interesting thought reminding us heaven is a very real and wonderful place.

Hurting people need to hear just how special this place is called heaven. Having something tangible to hope for can help bring them through the tough times. Of course the lost, the ungodly, the untouchables of our day especially need to hear what God has prepared for those who are willing to surrender their lives to Him. Caregivers who know and believe in heaven can offer tremendous comfort and encouragement to those they minister to.

When human reason makes no sense of the trials of life, this is when the reality of heaven becomes so important. There is a reason why you are here. Death is not the end of it all. It does make a difference how you behave, especially under stress. It matters to God. It matters in heaven.

But what exactly happens when I die? What is the sequence of events before eternity is ushered in? Will I face judgment? When do I get to be resurrected? These are important aspects of heaven and eternity and need to be looked at in greater detail.

CHAPTER 3

WHAT HAPPENS WHEN I DIE ?

Where Does My Body and Spirit Go To?

Death is the unnatural separation of the spirit from the body. It is followed by what is called the intermediate state. This is the condition of the soul while awaiting the resurrection of the body. I have had a few close to death experiences, especially during my world travels as a young man. Only once in my life have I approached the point where I felt my spirit was about to actually leave my body.

Pressure in my chest was becoming unbearable. The nurse suddenly asked my wife what my pain tolerance was like. She increased the medication. When she asked Gayle to leave the room and brought in the crash cart I thought to myself, Larry, this is it!

Lying in that hospital room awaiting open-heart surgery I had been worrying about my family. How would they mange if I died. Why hadn't I got my affairs in better order? Will the insurance pay for all this? I began praying again. Face to face with my own mortality I found myself joking to God about my situation.

"Lord, I know you wanted me to write a dissertation on heaven, but did it have to include going there? At least let me finish it first!"

I could feel the very presence of the Lord in the room with me. It was as if He reached down and patted my head in assurance.

"Don't worry about your family, Larry, I'll always take care of them. Anyway, I am not finished with you yet, I still have things I want to do through you."

The peace of God flooded my soul.

Peace in the pain! Unless heaven is real it just doesn't happen like this. The fear never goes away. But it did! And it wasn't just the medication. The peace and reality of heaven has stayed with me.

When the body dies and the spirit leaves, it remains separate from the body until the resurrection. This period between physical death and resurrection we call the intermediate state. So how long are we in limbo? When do I get to be resurrected?

Everyone's body, when it loses its spirit goes to the grave. The Bible refers to the body *sleeping* after death, awaiting either the return of Christ or the judgment day (1 Cor. 15:51). For most people the body simply decays in a burial plot and stays in the same place. But no matter whether you are buried, drowned or blown apart at death, each of the individual cells, with the DNA making you uniquely you, is somehow tracked by the Creator. They are brought together again at the resurrection.

Only the body therefore, remains in limbo. The spirit lives on either in hell (Luke 16: 22-23), or in the presence of God in heaven (Luke 23: 43). If you are a child of God, your body will sleep (not your spirit) only until Jesus returns to earth for His church at the rapture. If you have rejected the Savior prior to your death then your body remains in the grave until the Great White Throne judgment at the end of the millennium.   After judgment the unsaved suffer a second death and are sent into the Lake of Fire for all eternity (Rev. 20:5-6, 15).

Two kinds of resurrection are written about in scripture. The first (in quality) resurrection is for the redeemed to everlasting life in heaven. The second resurrection is for the unsaved to eternal damnation and separation from God (Luke 14:13-14; John 5:28-29). Several individuals were raised from the dead in the Bible, only to die again later and await the final true resurrection into eternity; the widow's son (1 Kgs. 17:21-22), the Shunamite's son,

(2 Kgs.4:32-36), the man thrown onto Elisha's bones (2 Kgs. 13:21), Jairus' daughter, Man of Nain, Lazarus, Dorcas, Eutychus, and many saints at Christ's resurrection (Matt. 27:52,53).

Christ's resurrection is the first in order, followed by the church at the rapture, then the saints and martyrs of the tribulation period. The second resurrection, of the wicked, is however, a single event.

What's So Important about the Resurrection?

Central to Biblical faith is the fact of the resurrection. For heaven to be a physical place there must also be bodily resurrection. Christ's resurrection confirms our salvation and our hope of heaven. It gives assurance that Jesus is God, in human flesh, and that the Father has accepted His sacrifice for mankind's sin. Unless He were the sinless Son of God He could not have overcome the natural laws of death and decay.

Without the resurrection, Christianity is just like any other religion and we are without hope (1 Cor. 15:12-23). No other religion claims a resurrected founder. Yet Christ did rise from the dead and everyone else, whether they want to or not, will be resurrected one day (Rev. 20:11-15).

Resurrection is a leading topic in the New Testament and a central part of the end-times teaching. We have already seen how nature itself hints at resurrection all around us. Our limited, sense and experience oriented minds want to reject the notion as being ridiculous. What is really ridiculous is Christian service if there is no resurrection.

You can't be a Christian and deny the resurrection of the body, for no one can be saved without believing in Christ's resurrection (Rom. 10:9). Unbelievers never do receive a new body even though they are resurrected. The redeemed on the other hand get to receive new glorified bodies at the rapture. Those who have died in Christ spend their intermediate time in some kind of temporary spiritual body.

Why do I believe we receive a temporary spiritual form if we die now? At the transfiguration both Moses and Elijah were seen by Peter, James and John and somehow they also recognized these patriarchs (Mark 9:4-5). They had human form, or at least appeared to the disciples that way, even though their clothing had a supernatural brightness to it.

At the rapture when Christ returns for His bride, the church, our present bodies will be instantly changed into glorified, perfect, physical bodies that will live for ever. This is why the apostle Paul longed to be out of this earthly body and with Christ (2 Cor. 5:1-10). In that day all the aches and pains and struggles of this aging body will be over, for good. Hallelujah!

Transformation of the old body into a new one is what the Bible teaches takes place (1 Cor. 15:51-53). The decay and graveyard sleep of the old body is interrupted and instantly transformed into an incorruptible body. There is nothing left in the grave.

For the unsaved, however, their dead bodies continue decaying until the end of the thousand year rule of Christ on earth, the millennium. God must keep careful track of all the elements of these bodies also. They come together and are resurrected at the end of the age. But these are not changed. The wicked will stand trial before God in their old, aching bodies of before (Rev. 20:12-13; Mark 9:43-44). But why does the Bible make it seem so complicated? Why the need for old and new bodies, raptures, and different kinds of resurrection?

Why Do Our Bodies Have To Die in the First Place?

Adam was created with a body that had the potential for immortality along with his spirit. A Holy perfect God created man in His own image to have fellowship with him, to glorify Him and enjoy Him for ever. The first couple blew this opportunity by choosing not to trust what God had said and to make their own decisions as to what was right and wrong (Gen. 3).

Unlike anything else in all creation, God had given mankind this freedom of moral choice. Without it we would have been just like the animals that live by genetically programmed survival instinct. We would have been robots. But God desired man to freely choose to love and trust Him so He could have even closer fellowship with him than with the angels. In fact Jesus' prayer in John 17 indicates God wants to be as close to all His children as He is with the Son and the Holy Spirit (John 17:21).

To remain true to Himself, Holy and perfect, God by His own nature cannot have fellowship with anything less than perfect. So the minute Adam and Eve sinned, the built in genetic potential for immortality was marred within them. From this moment on Adam and all his descendants became programmed to decay and death, physically and spiritually. Because the whole universe was created to sustain man, it too suffers the same physical inevitability towards decay and death (Rom. 8:19-22).

This is why our bodies die. Science tells us that for all the cells replaced each day within our bodies more of them die than are replaced. No matter how hard they try, scientists will never be able to reverse this process. This is why we need new bodies to live in heaven.

Man is also spiritually dead, separated from a Holy Creator. This is why Adam and Eve could no longer live and walk and talk with God in the garden of Eden. This is why we need to be born again in spirit in order to have fellowship with God again and be with Him forever in heaven.

What about Judgment?

Death is not the only consequence of man desiring to be master of his own destiny. Because we were made moral creatures in the image of God, there is a judgment day coming for all the moral choices we have made throughout our lives on this earth. Everyone will have to give account (Rev. 20:11-15). So how many Judgments are there?

Individuals who have not accepted Christ's sacrifice for their sins will be judged at the Great White Throne judgment at the end of the millennium. Nations will be judged at the end of the great Tribulation at Christ's second coming. Believers, the moment they trust in Christ are judged and acquitted of all their sin, past, present and future.

The believer's works (for Christ) will be judged at the Bema, or judgment seat of Christ(Rom. 14:10-12). The nations will be judged in relation to their support for or against Israel. Israel itself will be judged also at the second coming of Christ. Those Jews who waited for the true messiah (and not the antichrist) will be allowed into the millennial kingdom. There will be a final judgment of the angels also.

Records are kept in heaven on every person that's ever lived (Rev. 20:12). When the unsaved are brought to trial at the great white throne judgment these books are opened. Justice is finally meted out upon the wicked. Everything a person has ever said or done will be revealed on that terrible day and God will pronounce His judgment upon it.

What a frightening thought? Everything you have said and done on this earth is still happening in time and space. Science tells us every radio and TV wave is still out there somewhere, going on for ever. The light from approximately nine years ago has only just reached the nearest star (nine light years away). Theoretically this means if someone were looking at earth with a visual telescope from this nearest star, they would not see what's happening now, but what happened nine years ago.

Think about this for a moment. Everything you have ever done, good or bad, can still be seen somewhere out there in time and space. So it can certainly be seen by God. Ouch! Perhaps on that Great White Throne judgment day we will all see and hear, in living color and reality, everything which has happened in the past?

There will be no secrets. You will finally see the wicked from God's perspective and understand and applaud His just punishment. Then you will understand God does not send anyone to hell. The unsaved person deliberately chooses to spend eternity without God. They still want to be master of their own destiny and submit to no one. In pride they refused to accept God's free gift of forgiveness while on earth. Why? Because they didn't think they needed it.

Nobody consciously wants to go to hell. But many don't really want to go to a heaven of worshiping and serving Christ, no matter how perfect, prosperous or peaceful it may be. How arrogant to believe we know everything there is to know. How sad when men refuse to believe the word of the One who created them, and the offer of eternal life in His Son. How wonderful to think in Christ our sins are blotted out in time and space forever (Psa. 103:12). I don't understand how God does this. Perhaps He destroys them all instantly in a giant black hole (if these things actually exist). But my sins can't be seen or heard anymore.

What Happens at the Judgment Seat of Christ?

Recognition of things done for Christ while here on earth will be given at the judgment seat of Christ (1 Cor. 3:13-15; Rom. 2:6-10). Every believer will have to give an account of how he served the Lord and will receive awards for his faithfulness (Rom. 14:10-12; 2 Cor. 5:9-10). This judgment seat is called the Bema.

The Bema was a special military platform erected in ancient times. It was used to review the troops returning from a military triumph. Awards would be given from this platform to the conquering Commander and to those who had displayed exceptional bravery in battle. Captured slaves and the spoils of war were presented to the city and the commander-in-chief on this platform.

The Bema seat of Christ is very similar in that it is more for bestowing rewards than for rejecting failure. The point here is one of judgment of service not of sin to be punished. Bema holds no fear for the believer only joyful anticipation. In fact, I believe that we will be greatly surprised when we hear how many times Christ used us to touch other lives for Him and we weren't even aware of it. The cups of cold water given in His name will be recognized and rewarded.

The only regret might be from the believer's own recognition of missed opportunities and how much more they could have served the Lord. The only loss suffered here will be from the realization that much of what we told ourselves and others was done for Christ and in his name, were actually proud and selfish acts, done with wrong motives.

Just as at the ancient Bema seats the captured spoils were shared with those in authority, so we too will lay all our crowns at Jesus' feet (Rev. 4:10). Why would we do this? Because we will recognize without Him we can do no good, and only what we have let Him do through us counts for anything in eternity. So all the awards really belong to Him in the first place. It will be no loss for us for Christ has already promised to share all the inheritance and wealth of heaven.

What about the Intermediate State?

Paradise, the garden of God now within the city of God (Rev. 22:1-2), is where the dead in Christ will spend the time before the Bema event. Jesus promised the thief on the cross that he would be with Him in paradise as soon as he died. The intermediate state for the child of God will be one of great peace and rest and joy with Christ in heaven. It will also be a time of great anticipation of the events to come.

To be absent from the body is to be present with the Lord, Paul tells us. The intermediate state must therefore be spent in heaven for this is where Christ is, in heaven's throne room. It is not spent in some spiritual limbo waiting for a second chance to go to heaven. The Bible teaches there are no second chances after death. Your spirit is either in heaven or hell and it is impossible for it to cross over (Luke 16:26).

Regret and torment in hell will be the intermediate state for the unsaved. The account Jesus gives in Luke 16 tells us exactly what it is like. It is a place of unbearable heat and unbearable regret. The rich man in Jesus' story regrets not only his own condition in hell but fears his ungodly brothers, still alive on earth, will end up there just like him.

He is still selfish and arrogant, demanding Lazarus leave heaven to come to hell just to cool him down. Then, when this request is denied, he demands Lazarus leave heaven to return to earth to warn his brothers. He is still treating Lazarus like a beggar! Those in hell get to keep their old natures (Luke 16: 19-31)!

This passage clearly teaches during the intermediate state, whether in heaven or hell, we will live a conscious existence. Our souls (mind, will and emotions) will still be very much intact.

Samuel is the only person recorded in Scripture to communicate with someone on earth from his intermediate state (1 Sam. 28). The disciples on the mount of transfiguration saw Moses and Elijah in their intermediate state. The angels and God himself can of course communicate from heaven to those on earth. Any other supposed communications from beyond the grave can only be demonic.

The rich man in Jesus' story in Luke 16 was aware of what was happening in heaven and hell and even on earth. He was obviously unable to communicate with his brothers on earth. Peter, James and John could hear Moses and Elijah talking to Christ but they could not communicate with them, themselves. In fact as soon as Peter suggested such a thing, Moses and Elijah disappeared and God spoke from the cloud (Mark 9:4-6).

Our loved ones in heaven are aware of major events happening on earth just as the martyrs will be aware of God's judgments on earth during the Tribulation (Rev. 6:9-10). Aside from God's special dispensation, such as in the case of Samuel coming back to speak to Saul, there is no Biblical evidence of any communication from the dead. Even the medium of Endor was amazed and terrified Samuel actually appeared. She knew it was not due to any power of hers he appeared and spoke (1 Sam. 28:12).

Angels carry the believer into heaven, Jesus taught. Many saints down through the ages have seen angels just before they die. Some people even claim to have had an out of body experience and to have seen the Lord before they returned to their bodies and life again. Are these accounts simply delusions or demonic deceptions?

The Bible clearly teaches it is appointed once for man to die and afterwards comes the judgment (Heb. 9:27). This pretty much negates the stories of people dying, coming back to life, and having some kind of out of body experience in between.

What is the Sequence of Events after Death?

Heaven or hell is the immediate destination of the spirit once it leaves the body at death. Next comes the intermediate state. The believer spends it in the presence of Christ in the heavenly city to await the resurrection. The unbeliever spends it in the presence of Satan and his demons in hell to await the judgment.

At the return of Christ to earth for the church, the believer's spirit momentarily unites again with his old body in the grave. He is immediately resurrected and his body transformed into a glorious new one. Together with the raptured saints they reign with Christ on earth for a thousand years. The unbeliever remains in the intermediate state until the end of this millennium when he is reunited with his old body and resurrected for judgment.

After the judgment comes the new heaven and earth. Let's look then at what this new world will be like.

PART II.

A NEW WORLD

CHAPTER 4

THE NEW EARTH

Why Is Earth So Special?

Stars filled the blackness from horizon to horizon. Planets passed as we traveled through space. Asteroids and comets flashed by. A bright, beautiful orb in the distance drew closer and closer and larger and larger. Suddenly it filled our view, in magnificent, colorful, stunning contrast to every other object we'd seen . . . planet earth!

I settled back into my soft recliner at the Boston Planetarium and gazed in wonder at the astronaut pictures of earth taken from outer space. Even the evolutionist announcer spoke in hushed awe about this unique "jewel" in space, as he called it. The recorded voice continued to explain, in quiet amazement, that everything in the universe seems to sustain life on earth. Why is there nothing else out there even closely resembling this planet? Why is earth so special?

Of course he had no answers because he didn't believe in a Creator. From the wonder in his voice I had a suspicion he was pretty close to changing his view.

Though just a tiny dot in the ocean of the universe, the earth is indeed unique, according to the Scriptures. The whole of the universe was created for the sole benefit of man on earth. Why? Because man is the pinnacle of creation, uniquely made in the image of the Creator. Though the earth will go through many changes (because of man's sin) it's foundations last forever (Psa.104:5). Christ holds the title deed to earth (Rev. 5). He believes all of earth's inhabitants are worth dying for and the world worth redeeming.

Promises of a new earth are found in both the Old and New Testaments (Isa. 65:17-25; 2 Pet. 3:13). Isaiah looked forward to a very earthly paradise of vineyards and houses and tame animals. Peter looked for Christ's perfect, righteous kingdom on a renewed earth.

Many would dismiss Isaiah's prophecy as referring solely to the millennial kingdom. The context of the passage (v17) however, is the new heaven and earth, eternity. Yes, earth will be very much a part of heaven. Though it will be similar to what we are used to here, the new earth will be so much better than this one Isaiah tells us we will never again long for the "good old days." We won't even think about it anymore.

No, heaven is not just a golden city in the sky. There is going to be a wonderful new world for you to explore, build on, cultivate and enjoy forever. This earth was meant to last forever until mankind messed it up. When God first created it for us, He declared everything about it to be good, perfect in fact (Gen. 1:31). So why wouldn't the new earth be similar? Does this mean then this earth will remain? Well, yes and no!

Renewal of what man has messed up is God's primary plan and purpose for this earth we now live on. There are several major destructions and renewals of earth in Scripture. In each case the renewed world is very similar to before.

The Bible teaches the basic foundations (or design if you like) of this earth remain forever (Psa. 78:69; 104:5; Eccl. 1:4). When Adam sinned in the garden of Eden his fall affected all creation. The world he began to live in outside of the garden was basically the same world only now there were thorns and weeds and carnivorous animals.

Similarly, when God destroyed the world with water in Noah's day, the earth remained, though much of the topography, atmosphere and climate were changed. Yet it was still similar to what Noah had been used to with many of the same mountain ranges and rivers in place. In the same way, after the seven years of the coming Tribulation, the world, as we know it, will be destroyed by warfare, pollution and the supernatural judgments of God.

The earth and its basic systems are still there, however, at the second coming of Christ. The ecology will be restored during the millennium. Again at the end of the millennium when God destroys the earth (as we know it) with fire he will again restore and renew its basic form and systems only more gloriously than ever before. So, yes the earth remains, but no it will not be the same earth as before. It will be better!

Neos and *kainos* are the two Greek words for *new* in the New Testament. *Neos* refers to new in time (never seen before), and *kainos* to new in quality (renewal of what already exists). Throughout the book of Revelation, John consistently uses *kainos* when talking about the new earth.

Although Peter predicts the very elements will melt away when God destroys the world by fire, his use of *kainos* rather than *neos* points to a renewal or reforming of the earth, rather than a recreation from nothing (Pet. 3:10-13). Thus your future is going to be spent on a *kainos* earth, a new and improved version of the one that already exists. You see the Bible does have a much more "down to earth" view of heaven than you imagined. Are you saying then that heaven is not spiritual?

Is Heaven Earthly or Spiritual?

Peter looked forward to the fact this promised new earth would be one filled with righteousness(2 Pet. 3:13). The physical beauty of heaven is nothing compared to the spiritual beauty of a world filled with right-living people and the very presence of God. Ephesians tells us the blessings of heaven are primarily spiritual blessings (Eph. 1:3). Jesus' parables are filled with spiritual principles for spiritual living in heaven.

God is spirit and heaven now and heaven then is in a spiritual dimension, the same dimension as the realm of the angels, though there are, of course, physical aspects to it. Our glorified new bodies in heaven will be spirit controlled. Like Jesus after the resurrection we will be able to instantly go from the physical world to the spiritual and back again at will.

Because we are made in God's image, man is primarily a spiritual being (not sexual, as Freud maintained). We are only truly fulfilled when our spiritual needs are met. The primary joy of heaven is we will finally and forever be one with our Creator. All the material blessings will simply be fringe benefits.

Man has been given the physical earth to take care of, build on, cultivate and enjoy. It was made for him (Psa. 115:16). Heaven is God's dwelling place. The Bible presents this consistent dichotomy between heaven and earth. Heaven is always above and earth is beneath (Psa. 102:19).

God's throne is always above the earth. John sees the heavenly city, containing the throne room of God, coming down to the new earth (Rev. 21:2). He doesn't record that it ever lands on earth. If it remains in space above the earth then the Biblical dichotomy is maintained. God's dwelling place and the city He has prepared for His children to live in with Him is still above the new earth.

The new earth, as before, is for man to take care of, build on, cultivate and enjoy. Jesus, of course, as the God-man, will bodily and spiritually supervise all this activity on earth. It is part of His kingdom.

Types of heaven are all the way through the Bible. We will examine some of these in a moment. Each of these types gives us a taste of what heaven will be like. The hope of the Old Testament saints was heaven's city (Heb. 11:16). The hope and goal of the New Testament is heaven's kingdom (Col.1:5, 13).

Yes, the Bible does reveal much about what heaven will be like. All the things that the Scriptures say will last for ever, will obviously be in heaven and give us direct insight into what it will be like. The things the Bible tells us are in heaven now, such as angels, throne room, glory, joy and worship, give additional glimpses of what it will be like in eternity

The fact of heaven being by definition where God is, means everything you can learn about Him from the Bible also tells you what heaven is going to be like. The subject is endless. From Genesis to Revelation the Bible points to heaven and its King, Jesus. Thus a Biblical word study of such things as *glory, joy, power,* and *majesty* reveals much about heaven.

Abraham, as already mentioned, looked for a city in heaven. A special place he could settle in forever and never have to pitch a tent again. Throughout the Old Testament the Hebrews' longing for heaven was distinctly earthy. Read Isaiah's description and prediction (Isa. 65:17-25; 60: 5-22). Sure, both these passages refer to specific fulfillments in the millennium but notice the context of *forever* and *everlasting* in chapter 60 and the *new heavens* and *earth* of chapter 65.

Isaiah, Ezekiel, Micah, Zechariah and many of the minor prophets give detailed descriptions of the millennial kingdom which also have a forever context that points to heaven. The predominant Hebrew picture of heaven is one of peace and prosperity, sitting in your own bountiful vineyard in the promised land (Isa. 65:21-22; Mic. 4:4; Zech. 3:10).

What Bible Types of Heaven Are there?

Israel is a type of heaven, spiritually in the people of God, and physically in the promised land. The garden of Eden is a type of heaven, at least before the fall. It was a place where man walked with God. The millennial kingdom is another type of heaven, perhaps the closest description to the physical aspects of the new earth we have in Scripture.

Each of these types or patterns give you a clear taste of what heaven will be like. In fact, I believe they are meant to do just this, teach us about heaven and eternity. Everyone seems to assume that only John in Revelation gives any details on heaven. But in actual fact Revelation gives mostly details about New Jerusalem, the heavenly city, and barely mentions what the new earth will be like. It is all the rest of Scripture that does this. We just don't look for it because it doesn't mention the word *heaven* except in the context of God's throne above. But the heaven of eternity contains both the city and throne of God *and* a new earth.

Eden

Fellowship with God, on the old earth, was the essence and uniqueness of the Garden of Eden. It was an incredibly beautiful place. The garden and the whole world was meant to last Adam for ever. It was created to be eternal and so was Adam, hence the presence of the tree of life.   Even this tree, John tells us (Rev. 22:2), will also be in heaven.

Eden is a tremendous type of heaven because the world was perfect then. The descriptions in Genesis are therefore a pattern of what the new earth will be like. The vegetation, the animals, the birds, the rivers, the minerals and precious stones, the hills, the sea, the warm climate, and so on, are all similar to what is going to be in heaven.

The walking and talking daily with God, the closeness of human relationships, the joy of creative labor, will similarly be a part of heaven. You are still going to be able to enjoy all these things and more in eternity.

Israel and the promised land

Prosperity, peace and abundance was the hope of the promised land. God had promised Israel it would be a land flowing with milk and honey and eventually a place of rest (Deut.12:9-10). However, there was no peace at first.   Nonetheless it was a prepared land.   The cities and houses were already built, the fields cultivated, and the vineyards established.

As a type of heaven the promised land is not quite as close as Eden.   Though heaven is a land promised to God's people, and spiritually it now has to be battled for, in eternity there will be no enemies to fight, only perfect peace.   However, heaven is a prepared place.   The heavenly city is already built and waiting to be occupied.

The physical wealth and abundance of the promised land, the settling in tribes and families, the land ownership, the working and harvesting, the celebrations and worship, are all a pattern or taste of things that will be in heaven also. Israel itself, was established to be the primary type and pattern of the people of God.

The millennial kingdom

Land ownership, long life and enjoyment of family are some of the things predicted for the millennial kingdom. Prosperity, peace and perfect government under the Messiah is also a large part of millennial prophecy.   So, too, is a perfectly restored physical environment, including harmony in the animal kingdom as well as international harmony amongst men.

Having children, dying, the presence of sinners, and being protected from enemy nations are clearly predictions just for the millennium and not heaven. However, the Messiah's rule, which is so much a part of millennial predictions, is eternal. His kingdom continues on into eternity on the new earth also. So the millennium is a very definite type of heaven.

Thus you can be assured the environment in heaven on the new earth will be very similar to that of the millennium. The human activities will be similar also. Certainly there will be peace and prosperity, fulfillment and joy for everyone. Revelation even confirms the continuing presence and distinctions of nations (Rev. 21:24).

The Tabernacle

Perfection, in every detail, is the primary typology of the Old Testament Tabernacle and subsequent Temple. The Book of Hebrews tells us they were a pattern of the very throne room of God in heaven (Heb. 8:5; 9:23,24). The Glory of God's presence, though only once a year on the day of atonement, is another pointer to heaven. The precious stones, the gold and silver, the costly and colorful furs and skins used in the making of the tabernacle are types again of what will be in heaven.

Why are the instructions for the tabernacle so long and exact? Why are the penalties for not keeping to the letter of God's instructions so severe? To visibly demonstrate to God's people the Holiness of Jehovah God. John's picture of the throne room of God in Revelation is one of overwhelming Holiness, glory and awesome power.

God came down to His people once a year in the tabernacle. In heaven God's glorious presence will be forever with His people. Only the forgiven, washed clean, sacrificed for, and chosen of God could dare approach the Holy place in the tabernacle. Only those who by faith have been forgiven through the blood of the Lamb of God, Jesus, can enter heaven.

The tabernacle, and especially Solomon's temple later, were incredibly beautiful and costly structures. They are but a shadow of the magnificent temple city of God in heaven, New Jerusalem. But, I believe, they are also a pattern of the beauty, order and

41

magnificence of the new earth and the cities there we will live, work and rule over (Luke 19:17).

The church

Fellowship within the body of Christ, the local church, is a foretaste of what relationships in heaven and on the new earth will be like. The church is definitely a type of heaven, where believers can begin to experience a taste of heaven now. The church in its corporate worship is a type and foretaste of the activities of heaven and the new earth (Eph. 6:2).

As a young man I will never forget my first worship experience with fellow believers in a foreign country. Though I could not understand a word of the language I felt an immediate oneness of spirit with them as we sang and worshipped. Though they could barely understand my English, and knew very little about me except that I loved Christ, I was accepted like a long lost brother. They took me into their homes, even trusted me with their cars, and generally treated me like family.

It went far beyond polite hospitality. To enjoy such spontaneous love and trust with those with whom you could barely communicate was truly a heavenly experience.

The Biblical principles of church life as taught in the New Testament are very much a foretaste of what life will be like in the kingdom of heaven on the new earth. The order, authority, submission, trust, love, compassion, and joy of service prepare the believer for life in heaven. Strange as it seems to unbelievers, spiritual brothers and sisters within the church enjoy a closer relationship with one another than with their blood relatives who do not know Christ. It is a taste of heaven.

The sabbath

The Sabbath rest is a type of heaven too. We devote a whole chapter to this principle later. The church now, is Christ's spiritual kingdom on earth. It is a type of His physical kingdom in heaven. These are some of the major types so let's recap the order of them.

What Is the Progression of These Types of heaven?

Eden, the Sabbath, the tabernacle, the promised land, the temple have already occurred. We are currently in the church age which will end prior to the Tribulation years of God's judgment on Israel and the world. Then, at the end of those seven years comes Christ's return to earth to establish His millennial kingdom (the next type). At the end of this type and foretaste of heaven God finally ushers in the new heaven and earth.

Other things in Scripture, such as the river of God, Zion the city of God, and many of the promises and covenants of God, all point to heaven. Strictly speaking, anything about God, Christ and eternity in the Bible is a type and pointer to heaven. The major types we have briefly looked at give us perhaps the greatest insights into what heaven will actually be like for the believer.

So if there's going to be a new heavens (universe) as well as a new earth, what will it all look like? Will there still be stars in the sky? Will we still enjoy sunsets? Can I go to the moon or explore other galaxies? Let's look at what the Bible says about these things.

CHAPTER 5

WILL THERE STILL BE SUNSETS AND STARS?

What Is the Relationship of the New Earth to Space?

Navigating the oceans of the world before the days of satellites and GPS, the stars became familiar friends. If you have ever seen a night sky at sea near the equator then you know the majestic glory of the heavens. The stars are so thick everywhere you look, you can hardly pick out the constellations. Unless you are a navigator used to using a sextant!

Dusk after dusk and dawn after dawn you've braced your feet against the rolling deck, plucking little specks of light out of the sky and calculating them into perfect cocked-hat position lines on the chart. The stars were your friends. You could name them as soon as they appeared.

Often on lonely anchor watches at night in some far off foreign harbor I could dismiss the faint pangs of homesickness by just looking at the stars. Thousands of miles away mom and dad were looking at the same star I was. A little lower on the horizon maybe but the same star nonetheless. It brought both comfort and a sense of awe at the eternal majesty of the heavens. Oh, I hope there are stars in heaven! And there will be.

In my study of the Biblical words for *forever*, I discovered stars will still be very much a part of eternity (Psa. 148:3-6; Dan. 12:3; Jer. 31:35-36). In the creation account in Genesis we are told the sun, moon and stars are for signs and seasons as well as light (Gen. 1:14). Job, who apparently lived in the patriarchal period, long before the Law was given, was familiar with the constellations (Job 9:9; 38:31-32).

Perhaps, as has been suggested by other Bible scholars, the constellations are indeed signs of God. From the Lion of Judah to the virgin birth there is the message of God's love written across the sky. It's just that Satan has managed to distort and reverse the order of the message in the so called signs of the zodiac. Be this as it may, there will be stars in the sky and signs of God's glory in the new universe.

Genesis 1:1, the very first words of the Bible, reveal what science calls the time, space, matter continuum. In the *beginning* (time), God created the *heaven* (space), and the *earth* (matter). It is clear from the creation account the earth is the center of the universe, not physically but in its purpose and uniqueness. This time, space, matter relationship continues forever. The new heaven and earth will be just as before, the focus of the whole new universe.

But isn't this a bit medieval to say the earth is the center of the universe, in whatever sense you mean it? With all we have discovered about the vastness of space and the endless galaxies out there, how can you say the earth is even unique any more?

Yes, yes, I know all about the mathematical probabilities that suggest there must be similar or even advanced life forms out there somewhere. But we have not discovered everything yet (even about probabilities), nor do we fully understand everything we have discovered. If we had we would be God! And God has said that in the beginning He created the heaven and the earth (the universe) . . . and nothing else!

For the believer, this faith in what God has said about creation is crucial. If you just accept the scientific claim there must be other intelligent life out there, what does this say about the whole plan of salvation? God so loved the *world* the Bible tells us. John tells in his gospel that everything that is was made by Christ. In Him (Jesus) was life, and the life was the light of . . . aliens? No, of men (John 1:3-4).

In Him (Christ) all things exist (Col:1:16-17). He made the worlds, the other planets and galaxies (Heb. 1:9). Everything has been created by Him and for His pleasure (Rev. 4:11). Does He then have to die again for the aliens in outer space? No, of course not, because there are none. Sorry, if this breaks your little science-fiction heart. But realize what this means. You and I are the most important, intelligent, unique, and God-like creatures in the whole universe. You are also the most precious to God. And always will be in heaven.

Science fiction actually has nothing on the real thing. Heaven, where God and the angels dwell, is right here now, a fourth dimension we just can't see or access at this moment. The giant space-station city of God (New Jerusalem), which houses God's throne even now, will one day become the capital of the new universe.

Everything will relate to this city in heaven. It will be the power center for everything in existence. You will be able to access the New Jerusalem from anywhere in the universe or from the new earth. "Scotty, beam me up," will become a daily reality in heaven, as you return again and again to your mansion in the sky, and to the incredible worship center of God's throne room in New Jerusalem.

What and Where Is the Heaven of Heavens?

Paul was caught up into the present dimension of heaven. He describes it as the third heaven and also as paradise, the garden of God (2 Cor. 12:2-4). This threefold aspect (third heaven) we have already looked at. God's throne is in the third heaven or heaven of heavens, as Moses and Solomon describe it (Deut. 10:14; 1 Kgs. 8:23).

Where God dwells and rules the universe from His throne is the heaven of heavens. It has existed forever (Psa. 93:2), and is a place different from the atmospheric heavens and space. This throne room and the heaven of heavens becomes part of the New Jerusalem. When this happens we are not told exactly. But being the home Christ is preparing for His bride the church, this heavenly city probably began around the time of Christ's resurrection and His return to the Father. Certainly it was already constructed by the time John saw and wrote about it in Revelation.

47

What Will the New Universe Be Like?

Conservation of matter and energy is a principle we have seen already God keeps to. Though He himself is infinite, apparently He has chosen to conserve the limits of the universe. In our discussion of a *kainos* earth, even after the very elements of the universe melt, we have seen God prefers to reconstruct rather than annihilate and recreate.

Does this mean the new universe will have limits? Not necessarily. It simply suggests the new universe will be similar to the old, and that's pretty vast! The Bible does mention "from one side of heaven to the other," suggesting limits (Deut. 4:32), but in context it may refer to the boundaries of the throne room or the heavenly city. There certainly are limits to New Jerusalem. John gives us exact dimensions (Rev. 21:15-17).

Maybe the new universe will be curved, a closed system, as Einstein once suggested the present one is. Because of gravitational forces within the universe, he theorized if you started traveling away from earth in the same direction you would eventually come back to where you started. That's a little too much science for me to grasp, but it could still allow for a huge universe. Anyway, we will have an eternity to find out!

Supernovas in our present universe are exploding stars which have expanded to capacity. At least this is one of the current theories. Everything in space apparently expands, explodes and then contracts again into a black hole. So will the new universe expand or remain static? The Bible doesn't really say, only the new universe will be perfect and complete (cf Gen. 1:31-2:3). At present, even the galaxies and outer space have been affected by the Fall.

God knows the limits of His universe and this is all you need to know. This future dwelling place for mankind, heaven, is frequently described as a prepared place (1 Cor. 2:9; Heb. 11:16; John 14:2-3; Matt. 25:34). This again has the connotation of completeness. But God Himself, of course, is limitless and beyond finding out (Job. 11:7). This will be part of the fun of heaven, taking eternity to discover God and the answers to all these questions! Remember, too, you will have all the time in the world to explore the universe, no matter how large it is. Yet you will never get lost in it!

Creation already demonstrates how vast the universe is. When you consider the mind-boggling distances in space it is easy to believe in eternity. Our whole solar system is a tiny blip on the edge of a galaxy. They tell us too, there are a myriad more galaxies out there, most of them much larger than ours.

So will there be other galaxies in the new universe? Undoubtedly yes! *Kainos* new for the earth also applies to the heavens, the whole universe. This means it will be similar to what it was before. Following the pattern of Scripture promises for heaven, these galaxies will be even more wonderful than before. So will I get to explore them? Of course! They are created for our benefit and enjoyment.

Will We Travel in Space?

Space, and perhaps even time travel of some kind will be infinitely possible in heaven. We will talk in more detail about *time* later, but for now suffice to say that in your glorified body you will have the capacity to instantly transport yourself from place to place and from the physical realm to the spiritual.

How do I know that? Because you will receive a body just like Christ's, Paul tells us (Phil. 3:21). Christ was able to appear and disappear at will and transport himself instantly from place to place after the resurrection. Let's face it, Peter was made to walk on water in his old body. Imagine what Christ will enable you to do in your new one?

When the so called "natural laws" we presently observe can be superceded, what incredible, exciting experiences await us in heaven. Remember we will be perfect, glorified children of the Creator, with all of Christ's power available to us. Heaven is going to be absolutely awesome. It will be way beyond what science-fiction and Hollywood could ever come up with.

If you love the stars and are fascinated by space imagine the joy of having forever to discover what's out there. Perhaps in the physical realm you will even get to travel in some form of mechanical space craft. The creatures in Ezekiel 1, which parallel the ones John sees in Revelation 4, have winged and wheeled contraptions to apparently carry them around the throne room and take them from heaven to earth and back. Interesting? Oh, I know Ezekiel is describing spiritual creatures here in earthly terms, but he does indicate there are physical aspects to heaven and God's throne.

Will There Be Life on Other Planets?

God's purpose and plan in creating the universe is centered on mankind. The earth has been given to man to take care of, and to develop his own creativity in bringing glory to his Creator. In heaven it will be similar. The new earth and the heavenly city will be the center of creative activity in the universe. That does not negate the possibility of exploring and perhaps colonizing other planets and galaxies for the benefit of the new earth.

This perhaps begins to answer the question of whether there will be life on other planets. No! But there could be . . . when the saints from earth travel to these places and exercise their God given creativity. Who's to say? It's really just speculation at this point for the Bible doesn't address it specifically. But Biblical principles of eternity and God's purposes for man, give us a glimpse of what might be in heaven.

Whenever you pose the question of life being found other than on planet earth you also need to define what you mean by *life*. If you mean intelligent, human-like life, then clearly the Bible indicates no. If you mean life in terms of energy, movement, chemical reactions, then the universe is full of it.

Spiritual life is already out there, as we have seen. God, the angels, Satan and his demons, the saints in heaven and the spirits of the unsaved in hell are out there now. You just can't see them, communicate with them (except to God through prayer), or go to them. There are also cherubim and creatures like nothing you have seen on earth, ministering in God's throne room (Rev. 4: 6-9).

Outside of these, the Bible teaches, there are no other beings in space. In eternity, the unsaved together with Satan and his demons will be living in the Lake of Fire. If this is another specially prepared planet or star or is again, like the original hell, beneath the earth's surface, the Bible is not clear. What is clear is the fact it will be a place of conscious existence forever and ever.

Parallel to the physical world of earth we live in now are the spiritual realms. There is the spiritual realm of the heaven of heavens where God dwells and the spiritual realm between heaven and earth where the demons dwell. Satan is the prince of the power of this latter realm (Eph. 2:2). Just like the spiritual realm of heaven, which is all around you though you can't see it, so too is the realm of spiritual darkness.

Though we may try and rationalize it away, most of us experience the effects of this spirit world even though we can't see it. Do you really think that the evil deeds you see and hear of every day in the news are just random acts? No, they are spiritually orchestrated and controlled. The devil made me do it? No, he just gave someone the idea and they ran with it. The individual is still responsible.

Dare I suggest there are no random acts of love either. Heaven plans and orchestrates all of these too. If we neglect to do what the Holy Spirit prompts us to do God will find someone else or some other way to fulfill His purposes.

Ultimate power in the universe belongs to Christ (Matt. 28:18). He is the source of all power (Heb. 1:2-3). From heaven's throne room He rules the universe. John's vision in Revelation speaks of God's glory outshining the sun and lighting not only the heavenly city but the new earth beneath. Here in the throne room in the New Jerusalem will be the source of all power in the universe.

Christ will control everything from here, the people, the new earth, the stars and planets, the worlds beyond, His whole kingdom. If the glory of God's presence in the throne room is enough to light the earth, then does this mean the new earth will not have a sun?

Will There Still Be a Sun and Moon?

The sun, moon and stars last forever, the psalmist writes (Psa. 148:3-6; 72:17; 89:36-37). They will continue as long as Christ's kingdom, name, and throne! Jeremiah confirms the same thing (Jer. 31:35-36). Also, John in Revelation, Isaiah, Ezekiel, Daniel and other of the prophets consistently use the terms, *days, months,* and *years*, when referring to eternal prophecies.

Trees will bear fruit twelve months of the year in heaven (Rev. 22:2). The gates of the city will not be shut all *day* (Rev. 21:25), for there is no night or darkness within the city. A moon is required for months and a sun for days. Jeremiah in particular makes it clear that when God established these ordinances they will continue as long as Israel does. Along with the "grafted in" church, the true Israel continues forever.

Psalm 148 tells us the sun and moon have been established forever and ever. Psalm 89 tells us the moon will continue as long as Christ's kingdom. Yes, I believe the Bible teaches there will be a renewed sun and moon in heaven. But doesn't Revelation teach there will be no sun, that the Glory of God's light will replace it?

New Jerusalem will not need the light of the sun by day nor the light of the moon by night, for the glory of God will light it (Rev. 21:23). It says nothing about the new earth. "There will be no night *there* (in the city) . . . neither light of the sun (Rev. 22:5). It consistently talks about the fact the heavenly city does not *need* the sunlight, not that there is no sun or moon. We know too, within the throne room of the city, there is no direct sunlight (Rev.7:16).

It does talk about the nations walking in the light of the city (21:24), which could imply the city is so bright it lights the earth as well. In which case the presence of the sun and moon would then become primarily to mark the passage of time and the seasons rather than give light to the earth. However, verse 24 describes the leaders of these nations coming into the city. So "the walking in the light of it" could mean just when the nations are visiting New Jerusalem.

Either way, the Bible declares the sun, moon and stars will be renewed in heaven. Does this mean we will still be able to enjoy sunsets? Absolutely, and probably even more magnificent and beautiful than before.

Just as an interesting thought here. The sun's light is chemically generated light. The light of the moon and earth is only reflected light. The light of the glory of God is the source of all light. The light of New Jerusalem therefore, is where light itself begins. This would make this dazzling city the center of the universe. God brings this city down towards earth making the new earth now the actual (as well as purposeful) center of the universe. Not so medieval after all! So maybe the new earth becomes a satellite of New Jerusalem rather than the other way around?

Lightning, thunder and rainbows are present in the throne room of God, and plenty of water (Rev. 4:3,5). This suggests the continuance of an atmosphere or firmament of some kind in heaven. Along with the sun, moon and stars, the firmament or atmosphere is also declared to last forever (Psa. 148:3-6; Dan. 12:3). It's the moisture in the atmosphere which makes the sunsets so special.

The new earth will be incredibly beautiful, yet similar to before, so why wouldn't the sunsets be even more spectacular? The sun is used in Scripture as a picture of God (Psa. 84:11). The Messiah himself is referred to as the Sun of Righteousness (Mal. 4:2). I am sure sunsets will still reflect His glory in heaven.

So if we can enjoy sunsets on the new earth what else is in store for us there? Will there be mountains, oceans, animals? What about fish, reptiles and insects? Will there be cities and buildings there?

CHAPTER 6

WILL THERE BE MOUNTAINS, OCEANS, AND ANIMALS?

Will There Be Gardens in Heaven?

Unemployment can be a soul-destroying experience. Day after day scouring the want-ads, mailing out resumes, driving to interviews. Nothing pans out. Is it my lack of skills, education or experience? Or do I have some fatal character flaw? God, why am I here? What do you want me to do with my life? The beauty of a garden restored my sanity. A quiet touch of paradise finally brought peace and understanding.

It was a place called Edward's Gardens in the beautiful city of Toronto. Formally landscaped in a natural ravine, a gentle stream flows through the middle of this tiny, flower-filled haven. Walking through it you are unaware of how close you are to the city. It was one of my favorite places when we lived in Canada.

It was here God began to prepare my heart and thoughts towards the ministry. It was here, with gentle chipmunks and black squirrels for company, I wrote my first poem. Walking, writing, praying in a garden healed my soul.

It all began in a garden. It all climaxes in a garden . . . the garden of God, paradise, heaven. Maybe it's just my British heritage but I love formal, flower filled gardens. I have visited many of them all over the world and they always make me feel close to my Creator. Yes, the heavenly city has a formal garden in it, with a river flowing through, its banks lined with trees that bear fruit every month of the year (Rev. 22:1-2). Will there be gardens on the new earth? Most definitely, so let's look at what this new earth will be like.

Order, balance, function, symmetry, is evident in all of God's creative work. He created the earth as a circle, or globe (Isa. 40:22; Pr. 8:27). We have already seen the foundations of the earth, though they will be shaken and reformed, remain forever (Psa. 104:5; Eccl. 1:4). So this beautiful globe, this precious jewel in space, will remain as a globe in space forever.

Given what we have seen already of God's penchant for conservation, the new earth will most likely be the same approximate size as before. Won't we need a larger earth to sustain all the millions of saints that will be there? Isn't the earth now so overcrowded, soon there won't be enough to go around?

Our present problem is not lack of resources or space. There is plenty to go around. Rather it's our selfish misuse of the abundance all around us causing the alleged dilemma. You could fit the whole five billion population in the State of Rhode Island, and each family would have more space than most of the people have now in Mexico City.

Heaven, remember, consists of more than just the new earth. There is the huge heavenly city. Given the size of New Jerusalem it will easily house the whole population of heaven on its own. Yes, the new earth will be plenty large enough, and as before will teem with life and abundance.

What Will the Climate Be Like?

Extremes of temperature or climate were unknown in the garden of Eden. There was no rain either. Instead a gentle mist watered the ground each day (Gen. 2:6) from the waters above the firmament (atmosphere) (Gen. 1:6-7). This suggests the world back then had some kind of uniform subtropical climate under a canopy of moisture.

Adam was originally without clothes so there were no extremes of cold, just a cool, gentle wind in the morning and evening hours when he would walk with God (Gen. 3:8). After Adam was kicked out of the garden we do read hard work began to make him sweat (Gen. 3:19).

Of course, all of the destructions and renewals of the earth given in Scripture changed the climate dramatically. Will the earth return to an Eden like existence? Unfortunately Scripture only hints as to what the climate will be like. We know in New Jerusalem no one will suffer sunburn (Rev. 7:16). We know too an atmosphere of some kind exists in heaven. This suggests the earth's climate will be very similar to what it is now but perhaps without the extremes.

Isaiah's picture of the millennial kingdom and of the new earth is one where nothing in nature hurts God's people anymore. This includes the climate also. God's promise to Noah of continuing seasons, cold and heat, seedtime and harvest, gives us another clue (Gen 8:22). Though the world as Noah knew it will once again be destroyed, its basic design remains forever. The millennial typology of planting and harvesting will continue on the new earth, so also, therefore, will the seasons.

Thunder and lightning, dark clouds and hail and even a rainbow are seen in heaven (Rev. 4:3, 5; 11:19). Throughout the Bible, in Job, Isaiah, Ezekiel, the Psalms and Revelation, there is recorded a firmament (or atmosphere with clouds) to be in heaven. Clearly there will be some weather patterns therefore on the new earth.

The major difference will be, there will be no destructive weather patterns. They will be orchestrated from the throne to bless the earth so it can bring forth its abundance. This will apparently be according to the seasons. Christ exercised power over the weather and we may be given such power on the new earth also.

Weather in the Bible is often used by God as a form of judgment. This will no longer be necessary in heaven. However, it is interesting to note what we would presently consider violent weather phenomena (thunder and lightning) is an integral part of the glory of God in His throne room (Rev. 4:5). God's voice is heard in the power of nature and when it occurs on earth now, the angels in the throne room give praise to God's glory (Psa. 29). The awesome power of nature on the new earth will still cause us to give glory to God. It just won't harm anything or anyone anymore or cause us any fear.

Will There Be Mountains?

Flooding of the whole world in Noah's day did not destroy all the mountains (Gen. 8:4). Nor did it destroy all the river beds. The Euphrates for one, was there in Eden (Gen. 2:14), and is still there now! Jacob and Habakkuk both describe the mountains and hills as being everlasting (Gen. 49:26; Hab. 3:6). Specific hills such as Mount Zion continue forever (Psa. 68:16; 125:1).

There will be hills and mountain ranges on the new earth for all eternity. They will still be feeding the rivers with rain and melted snow. There's another hint at the climate? The mountain ranges may well be very different, as I am sure they were after the devastation of the flood. The terrible destruction of the Tribulation judgments and the battle of Armageddon causes islands and even mountains to disappear (Rev. 16:20). But we know Mount Zion and the Mount of Olives remain.

The mountains may be rearranged a little, probably with even more spectacular peaks and grand canyons than before. The new world will still be an awesome place for us to explore. The magnificence of the vistas will once again cause us to continually praise God.

Will There Be Seas?

Rivers run from mountains to the sea. There are rivers in heaven so there are probably seas also. The Psalmist tells us the earth was founded on the seas (Psa. 24:1-2). · The foundations (basic design) of the earth last forever (Psa. 104:5). God said the sea was good (Gen. 1:10).

We've seen the atmosphere lasts forever. The moisture of atmospheres comes from seas. Ezekiel's millennial vision points to the eternal kingdom and the garden of God in its close parallel with Revelation 22. Here is another example of the sea continuing in eternity (Ezek. 47:8). There is also a sea in the throne room of God (Rev. 4:6; 15:2).

But don't some Bible commentaries tell us there will be no sea in heaven? Yes, I know, but this is based on just one little phrase in the Book of Revelation. John indeed writes that "there was no more sea" (Rev. 21:1). But let's examine this closer. The word

John uses for *more* here is a very common Greek term *eti*. When used with a negative (no), it can mean *not yet*, or even *no further* (Mk. 14:63), as well as no more or no longer.

Even when translated *no more* it does not always mean a definite ending. Jesus told His disciples He would see them *no more* (John 16:10), meaning no more on earth, not that they would never see him again in heaven. Thus this phrase about, no more sea, could legitimately be translated *no further* (additional) sea, or even *not yet* any sea. Remember, too, the sea was John's prison bars, exiled on the island of Patmos. He was probably glad to see these familiar seas pass away together with the first earth and first heaven (Rev. 21:1).

I know I have been a bit technical here and maybe even a little biased, because I love the sea. But so did Jesus. He spent half His ministry traversing the Sea of Galilee or walking and teaching from its shores, as well as in towns on the Mediterranean Sea. It is the rest of Scripture's emphasis on the foundational importance of the seas which convinces me they will be reformed again in heaven. I find it interesting too, when the earth was destroyed by the flood, the Bible does not mention life in the sea being destroyed (Gen. 7:21-23). The sea, with its teeming life forms, will be there again in eternity.

I firmly believe, from my study of the Bible, everything about creation which has been enjoyed on this earth, which has awed man and caused him to praise God, will be reformed even more magnificently than before on the new earth, along with wonders and pleasures as yet unimagined.

Palm trees, fir trees, myrtle and fruit trees are seen to be in heaven (Rev. 7:9; 22:1; Psa. 46:4; Isa. 55:13). There will be grasses and grapes but no thorns. Isaiah, Ezekiel and the Psalmist in particular paint a glorious picture of the new earth to come. Pastures will be covered with flocks, valleys covered with corn, and even the hilltops producing grain. (Psa. 65:13; Isa. 35:2; 55:12).

The natural wonders of this earth we enjoy now, and the promised millennial kingdom to come, are a taste of what will be in heaven. It will be the same only more beautiful and perfect than ever before, with all creation once again declaring God's praises. For the saints in heaven, the new earth will be a glorious, peaceful, abundant world to live in forever.

Will There Be Animals in Heaven?

Horses have always been a part of heaven, from the chariots of fire and the angel armies, to the white horse John sees Jesus riding at His return to earth. Though these may seem more symbolic than actual, remember Jesus is now physically in heaven and physically returns to earth. There will be animals in heaven. Isaiah's beautiful picture of the wolf and the lamb feeding together confirms this fact (Isa. 65:25). Remember, in context, Isaiah is not just talking about the millennial kingdom, but is also pointing to the new heaven and earth of eternity.

God created the animals and declared them good (Gen 1:25). They are a pattern and taste of what will be in heaven. They were made for man's benefit and for him to have control over. God brought every animal to Adam for him to name. Adam must have had a tremendous rapport with those creatures. God brought all the animals to Noah to take care of in the ark. Noah also, must have had a special way with animals.

Jesus had a special way with animals too, of course. He quietly rode an unbroken colt. We will be like Him in heaven. So all you animal lovers out there can look forward to an eternity filled with beautiful tame creatures to enjoy forever.

I wonder if we will be able to communicate with the animals in heaven? After all, even a disobedient prophet (Balaam) was able to once (Num. 22:27-30). Animals do have personalities (will and emotions) and maybe even minds, if Balaam's donkey is any indication. But they don't have spirits. No! You won't see "Rover" in heaven. You will see, I'm sure, a thousand pets just like him . . . and they won't ever die!

Sin caused animals to become carnivorous, Romans 8 tells us, man's sin that is. In Eden the animals were all vegetarian. In the millennium and on the new earth they will be vegetarian once again. So no living creature will ever die in heaven. There is no death anymore. Jesus has destroyed it (1 Cor. 15:26).

Isaiah sees the lion eating straw and snakes eating dust. Snakes in heaven? Apparently so, but they will not harm anyone, and impossible as it may seem to some of you, you will not be afraid of them! Perfect love casts out fear. You will be perfect in heaven. You will enjoy perfect love for God, and for all his creatures. After all, aren't you presently afraid of lions too?

Creeping things are another of God's creatures that many of us presently detest. Will they be in heaven also? The Bible isn't clear on this one. What is clear is that nothing on the new earth will harm us or make us afraid. It will be a perfect world.

Insects are used often in Scripture, both for judgment (locusts, flies, etc.) and for example (ants, spiders). They too were declared to be good. Some of them were even sanctioned as food . . . ugh! (Lev. 11:21-22). Like everything else in creation, a close study of even these creatures, reveals the marvel and glory of God's handiwork. They may well be in heaven.

Ezekiel sees fish in heaven. As the seas teemed with life before they will teem with life again in heaven. We haven't even seen all there is to see under the ocean yet. I am sure God will allow us to explore this world also in eternity. Once again it will be even more wonderful than before. What an incredible world we have to look forward to.

I encourage you to read in the book of Job. Especially chapters 37 through 41. God never does answer the *whys* of Job's terrible trials. Instead He simply and powerfully reminds Job of who He is, as seen in the world He has made for man. The descriptions of the weather, the sea, the sea creatures, and all of the animals and birds will stir your heart. It will (or should) cause you to want to praise our creator God.

If all these things helped Job to find out God then they are going to be in heaven also, or things very similar.

Will We Need to Cultivate the Ground?

Adam worked physically in the garden of Eden to keep it beautiful. He also worked creatively in naming all the animals. He was one smart guy. Work was not a curse until Adam sinned. Then it became hard, unrewarding, and survival necessary work

(Gen. 3: 17-19). Even in Eden before the Fall, the ground still needed to be tilled (Gen. 2:5).

The new earth therefore will also be worked and cultivated. The presence of domestic (work) animals in heaven (and the millennium) suggest this (Isa. 65:25). There will be no thorns or weeds. It will be a joy to do it. From the prophets to the psalms the vision of eternity is one of joyous planting, harvesting, and families feasting together on their own land (Psa. 65:13; Isa. 55:12; Ezek. 28;26; Amos 9:13-15).

The heavenly city, New Jerusalem, is already prepared for us. We will not have to work or build there, only fellowship with one another and worship the Lord together. The new earth, however will be for us to demonstrate our creative talents as we cultivate and settle this new world in eternity. This Biblical dichotomy mentioned before is thus maintained.

Promises of reward for faithful stewardship in Jesus' parables, indicates there will be cities on the new earth (Luke 19:17). Yes, there will be buildings there, and great cities too. Imagine being able to start from scratch, having all the resources and all the talented people necessary, to plan to build a city. Money will be no object, time will be no object, and there will be a perfect environment to work in. What architectural wonders will be in heaven, all blending beautifully with their surroundings. Of course I'm sure we will borrow a few ideas from New Jerusalem.

As we will examine later, there will be countries and nations in heaven, each with their own distinctiveness. The diversity of culture (minus the pagan religious influences) will again declare the glory of God. Are you beginning to see everything on this earth that brings you joy and reflects the glory of God is but a taste of what it will be like in heaven.

Nations bring the best of their cultural glories as gifts for the heavenly city (Rev. 21:24). The new earth must therefore be somehow divided up into countries and maybe even continents again. The Noah flood may well have triggered the original continental drift at the time of Peleg (Gen. 10:25). The earthquakes, falling meteors and general upheavals of the Tribulation may rearrange the continents once again (Rev. 6:14).

After the destruction of the world by fire at the end of the millennium, things will be different yet again. Given the recurring typologies for heaven in Scripture, I suspect the new earth will be quite similar to the present one in terms of major countries and continents. Countries and nations come and go in history, but some remain throughout. Which countries God will consider to enter into eternity is another whole study. Rest assured you will be an integral and important part of one of them.

How Will We Travel the New Earth?

Jesus in His resurrection body walked the Emmaus road. He walked the shores of the sea again with His disciples. He probably also went sailing again with them. Man was created to walk. In fact the medical profession tells us walking is one of the best forms of healthy exercise. We were undoubtedly a much fitter race before the advent of cars, and planes, and trains.

Jesus also transported himself instantly from place to place after the resurrection. We have already talked about this form of spiritual transportation. Walking will be a joy on the beautiful new earth, especially when you won't get tired. Instantly beaming up to New Jerusalem will be exciting too. But how else may we travel from country to country on the new earth?

We have already seen the strange transports the cherubim use in Ezekiel. With mankind's God given creativity there may well be all kinds of physical transports developed for the new earth. Under Christ's rule on this new earth any form of transport will carefully use the natural resources without pollution or destruction. If you have ever dreamed of owning a new Mercedes or Porche, or maybe even your own private plane, just wait till you see what's parked in the driveway of your new home in heaven? This magnificent machine, with its pollution-free propulsion, will never wear out!

Perhaps you think I'm being too speculative here and using too much imagination. Where does it say that in the Bible? Well, of course it doesn't specifically. Yet Scripture clearly teaches there will be houses and physical buildings in heaven so why wouldn't there be physical means of transportation? After all, Elijah entered heaven in a chariot! I tell you, this place is going to be awesome.

Have you ever taken a vacation you wished would go on forever? Have you ever arrived at a beautiful new resort and thought how awesome it would be to actually live there? This is just a taste of what the new earth will be like.

But what about the heavenly city, the New Jerusalem? Are the streets really gold? How big is it? What shape is it? Will I enjoy living there?

CHAPTER 7

GOD'S DAZZLING SPACE STATION

Are the Streets really Gold?

Driving directly into the sun on Dallas's northern ring road it was hard to keep in lane. The traffic, as ever, was fierce and fast and my sunglasses were of little help. Topping a sudden rise in the road we were startled by an amazing sight. Curving away to the left was a city of pure gold!

A complex of high, glass office buildings were reflecting the golden rays of the setting sun. No visible concrete, barely discernable steel framing, just sheer wall after wall of transparent, golden glass slid by us on the highway. From close range we saw much of the glass was actually gold tinted, and even the gray glass appeared gold in the reflected sunlight.

From a distance, and just for a moment they looked like solid gold buildings but up close they were obviously transparent. What a sight! Now I know what John must have felt like when he first saw the heavenly city. "And the city was pure gold, like unto clear glass" (Rev. 21:18).

John describes Main Street in the same way, the road itself, that is (Rev. 21:21). How can you have pure gold that's transparent? Remember the astronauts walking on the moon? What was it they had on their transparent visors to protect their eyes from radiation? That's right, a coating of pure gold.

Heaven's refining techniques are, I am sure, much more advanced than ours. John says it was *like* glass but *is* pure gold. Amazing, isn't it? What we now consider a precious metal, to be worn as jewelry or stored in a vault, will in heaven be used to walk on! Which gives you an idea of the values of heaven and how spotlessly clean this city will be.

Huge walls surround this golden city. Almost 20 stories high they are made of jasper. Perhaps the closest thing to today, to John's jasper, would be a diamond. Imagine a wall over two hundred feet high made of diamonds surrounding a gold city that has the light of God's glory shining through it? Shining buildings encircled with sparkling walls (Rev. 21:9-21).

I love how it was described by a radio preacher I once heard. He said the heavenly city would appear as diamonds set in gold, like a giant engagement ring in space, a symbol of Christ's love for His bride, the church.

Within these diamond walls are 12 entrances, gates of pearl, three on each of the four sides of the city. Each gate has an angel guard, and each gate has written on it a name of one of the 12 tribes of Israel. This is the city God has prepared for them (Heb. 11:16). Entrance into this city comes only through faith in the Messiah of Israel, Jesus. The gates are perpetually kept open. Each gate appears as one pearl, either pearl shaped or covered in pearl.

The city wall is built on 12 foundations, each engraved with the name of one of the apostles. Through these apostles, who founded the church, the gentiles now have access to this city. Through faith in the Lamb of God, the Jewish Messiah, gentiles are grafted into the true olive tree of Israel (Rom. 11:17-24).

How Was the City Designed?

Design of this city is unlike anything ever yet built on earth, because its designer is God. He has already prepared and built it with transparent gold and precious stones. These materials are clearly (excuse the pun!) intended to allow the light of God's glory to shine through them. Even the foundations are inlaid with 12 different precious gem stones, the same stones found in the High Priest's breastplate (Exod. 39).

These gem-stones at the base of the walls are an incredible mix of reds, blues, greens, yellows, purple, and white. Together with the diamond-like facets of the walls themselves, the light from within the city would be broken into all the colors of the rainbow around the dazzling gold of the city buildings. What a blazingly bright and breathtakingly beautiful city this will be. Neon lights and gold-tinted skyscrapers pale into insignificance beside it.

How was it all put together? Before the foundation of this world God prepared the kingdom of heaven for us (Matt. 25:34). Jesus did tell His disciples He was going to prepare a place for them, so there is a definite point in time when the actual city of New Jerusalem came into existence.

Jesus was a carpenter while on earth, so I like to imagine the interior of these golden buildings have the most exquisite woodwork within them. Whatever the inside of the buildings are like they will each be personalized to satisfy even the grandest dream-home desires you have ever imagined. Christ is the bridegroom of the church and in love will prepare the perfect home for us.

Dimensions of the city are huge. It is about 1500 miles wide, deep and high (Rev. 21:16)! Obviously there would be many levels, given the height of the city, which means there is more than enough room for mansions for everybody. If it came down and rested on earth its height would make it seem grossly out of place, and God is a God of order and symmetry.

Its base would cover two thirds of the United States, or all of Europe, or the whole Middle East, and some. It is the height of the city that intrigues me. 1500 miles high is 250 times the height of Mt. Everest! This means if the city were resting on earth its top would reach into outer space! Unless the new earth is much, much larger than before, and we have seen already this is unlikely, the New Jerusalem must remain in some kind of orbit around the earth. Or, of course, the earth now orbits around the city of God.

What Is the Relationship of the City to Earth?

Space stations and biospheres are enclosed self-supporting environments man has attempted to develop with minimal success. Trying to devise a completely recyclable system has produced more problems that it has solved. John, in Revelation, never sees the heavenly city land on earth or become part of it. He only sees it coming towards earth like some giant space station. This dazzling space-station city concept would maintain the Biblical dichotomy between heaven (in this case New Jerusalem), and earth (the new earth). God's throne, heaven, would still be above the earth!

I like the idea of earth then becoming a satellite of New Jerusalem. Indeed the whole universe will probably revolve around this power center. As far as creating a completely self-supporting environment, God already did this with earth. Building a self-supporting city in space for the saints to live in would pose no problems for Him.

This space station of God is unbelievably large. Do the math! Assume, say, a quarter mile square lot for each mansion, and levels every quarter mile, this would accommodate over two trillion homes! It would take a couple of million years just to drive by all the homes in heaven! The Bible teaches only a minority of the human race will make it to heaven (many are called but few are chosen, Matt. 20:16). The vast majority choose to spend eternity their own way, alone and separate from God. So the city won't need that many mansions. The accommodations are going to be enormous.

What Is the Shape of the City?

Foursquare is how John describes the shape of the city. The assumption is the New Jerusalem is therefore a cube shape. The whole city of New Jerusalem is the temple of God, a pattern for the earthly tabernacle and temple. In which case the city would be rectangular. John Walvoord, in his book The Millennial Kingdom, suggests another shape for the city, a pyramid.[2]

So which is it? Foursquare is essentially a two dimensional military term referring to a fortified city having four walls around it. It has more to do with length and breadth than height. In the Old Testament the dimensions of the tabernacle altars and high-priest's breastplate were indeed foursquare but not cubic.

---

[2]John F. Walvoord, The Millennial Kingdom (Grand Rapids: Zondervan Publishing House, 1959), 326-327.

Ezekiel's vision of the millennial temple again is foursquare but not cubic. The only cubic dimensions to be found are those of the inner sanctuary of Solomon's temple (1 Kgs. 6:20).

Walvoord's concept, therefore, of a pyramid shaped city has some merit. The city of God is constantly referred to in Scripture as Mount Zion, the hill of God, the mountain of God (Psa. 68:16; Ezek. 43:7; Heb. 12:22; Rev. 3:12). The pyramid is a perfect mountain shape. A 1500 mile pyramid in space, viewed from the new earth, would certainly appear as a giant mountain.

Satan of course, as the counterfeiter of all that is Godly, apparently loves to use this pyramid shape. From the giant tombs dedicated to the false gods of ancient Egypt, to the signs and symbols of new-age societies and the new world order, the pyramid is one of Satan's favorite emblems.

However, there is no clear precedent of a pyramid shape in the Bible. The predominant dimensions relating to the tabernacle and temple are rectangular, if not cubic. Read Revelation 21, and draw your own conclusions. I, for one, like the idea of a pyramid. It is one of the most stable structures in engineering and each face of this pyramid city would then reflect the strength and unity of the Trinity.

Christ, from His throne at the apex or center of this city, is the focal point of New Jerusalem. His glory not only lights the city and possibly the new earth as well, but it powers the whole universe. Light energy begins in Him. Jesus is the light. All power is given to Him. Everything in existence is sustained by His power.

The throne room, then, of this city of God is the center of all life. The ultimate source of water and life proceeds from the throne (Rev. 22:1). Jesus is also described as being the Word (John 1:14). Thus He is the source of all information for the universe. In our information age, Christ as the Word becomes even more relevant.

Since the advent of DNA discoveries and genetic engineering, life has been redefined as "the information (chemical code) necessary to create and sustain a living organism." So life is now genetic information (at least according to the scientists). They tell us within any cell of my body is enough genetic information to produce a complete me, from my toes to my hair! Wow! Let's think about this for a minute.

From a human perspective how is information communicated? Primarily by words. Oh, I know computers communicate with a code of zeros and ones, but these only make meaningful sense to humans when transposed into words. If Christ is the Word, He is the ultimate source of all information (genetic or otherwise) of everything that exists. In Him and Him alone exists the power to create and sustain everything and everyone. He spoke (words) and the world came into being. And it all proceeds from His throne in the city of God. He, Jesus, powers the universe. He is the Life (John 14:6).

So What Is in this City?
Buildings, streets and a garden are within the city walls as well as a throne room. John mentions only the (main) street of the city but presumably there are countless other golden streets, given the immense size of the place. Jesus talked about the dwelling places he was preparing there and John sees a beautiful garden watered by the river coming from the throne.

We have already seen there are trees and fruit there and of course countless angels as well as saints. There will be libraries of books, records, documents of everyone and everything related to redemption (the Lamb's book of life) and earth's history, and of course copies of God's word (Psa. 40:7, Phil. 4:3; Heb. 12:23; Rev. 5:1; 13:8; 20:12).

Within this vast city will be the mansions and homes individually prepared for God's people. Everyone's primary dwelling will be here, though there will be other homes, land and possessions on the new earth. John sees no separate temple building within the city (Rev. 21:22). There is no need of a separate place for God's presence. This is His home. Indeed the throne room and the whole city are the temple of God (Psa. 11:4; Isa. 6:1;Rev. 11:19; 16:17).

There is fire, and lightning and clouds, a river and a lake within the city (Rev. 4:5,6). There are animals too, in this city, horses and also strange creatures within the throne room that Ezekiel identifies as Cherubim. The fact of engraved names being on the gates and foundations indicates this city will be well signed. You will never get lost here.

There will be musical instruments and great treasure here in the heavenly city. It will be a wonderful place to explore. Just as we store and display great works of art and history and priceless treasure of this world within our major cities, so I am sure New Jerusalem will have treasures and wonders untold for us to admire. None of it will need rust protection or security alarms.

Just think of the most exciting and beautiful city you have ever explored. Now imagine for some reason you were given the keys of this city and were allowed access to everything and everyone, everywhere, at no cost. This would be just a taste of what life will be like in the heavenly city. We have been given the keys of the kingdom (Matt. 16:19; 18:18)!

Christ's physical presence is in heaven now. He is sitting at the right hand of the Father interceding for believers on earth. He is also walking in the city garden (paradise) with our loved ones that have gone on before us. Christ's physical presence will be there again when we all get to heaven. We have already seen there are angels guards at the gates of the city. There are special worship angels in the throne room and a multitude of other angels within the city serving the needs of the saints.

There will be both Jew and gentile believers within the city. Hebrews 11, and the names on the gates and foundations remind us this city was built for God's people Israel. In eternity the church and Israel become one family of God, the true Israel of faith. Given the marriage feast of the Lamb and the indication of continuing family feast and celebrations, there must be huge, magnificent banqueting halls within the city.

Which means there will be enormous kitchens there to prepare these feasts, together with culinary skills and delights you cannot begin to imagine. I don't think we will simply snap our fingers and turn stones into bread just for our own satisfaction, though that may be possible to do in heaven. Yes, it will be a real city with everything we would expect to be there in a world-class metropolis, similar yet vastly superior to all that we enjoy now. I can't wait to go there!

What Is the Name of the City?

Zion is another name used for the heavenly city, especially in the Psalms. Shalom, as most people know, is a Hebrew word for peace. Jeru-shalom, means city of peace. It is called *New* Jerusalem to distinguish it from the present earthly city and the refurbished city of the millennium.

This heavenly city is also known as the city of God, the city of the Lord, and the Holy city. Melchizedec (meaning "king of righteousness," a type of Messiah) was the king of Salem to whom Abraham paid tithes (Gen. 14:18). Salem is a transliteration of the same Hebrew word for peace. Salem is believed to be the same location as the subsequent city of Jerusalem.

Significantly, Abraham found in Salem a priest of Jehovah (Melchizedec) in the promised, but then pagan, land of Canaan. The future city of David, Jerusalem, was already being prepared spiritually in the promised land for God's people. The New Jerusalem is already being prepared physically in heaven for God's people. Faithful believers will have the name of this city displayed upon them (Rev. 3:12), probably on some special article of clothing similar to the way in which Jesus has His name written on His (Rev. 19:16).

Glimpses of the throne room of the city have been seen by several people in both the Old Testament and the New. We know God's throne has existed forever and the spiritual realm of heaven has too (Heb. 1:8). The 70 elders on the mountain of God in the wilderness saw the throne and the glory of heaven, so too did Daniel, Ezekiel, Isaiah, Jeremiah and others. Only John gives specific details about the city that now surrounds God's throne, though David prophetically points to it in several of the Psalms (eg. Psa. 48).

We know therefore the heavenly city, the physical one prepared for the saints, was in existence by the time John wrote Revelation. Paradise, the original one in Eden was not destroyed, simply hidden from mankind. Given the garden of God description in

New Jerusalem, paradise was probably translated from the realm of earth to the realm of heaven when Christ rose from the dead. John sees trees of life in the garden of New Jerusalem pointing to Eden itself being reformed in heaven.

Jesus promised the thief on the cross He would see him in paradise that very day. Paul, some years later, is shown paradise, which he also describes as the third heaven, the abode of God. To be absent from the body is to be present with the Lord so we know believers who die are instantly translated into the throne room of God and into paradise, the garden of God.

Both of these entities are now part of the heavenly city, New Jerusalem. So, yes, the city of God exists today and, yes, we get to go there when we die. But, no, we don't get physical bodies to fully enjoy the delights of this city until the resurrection and rapture. And, no, we don't receive our material rewards until the subsequent Bema seat of Christ. So what are our loved ones doing now in heaven?

In their temporary spiritual bodies their are enjoying peace and rest in the presence of Christ and His angels. They are also enjoying reunion and fellowship with other believers in heaven. Joy and laughter, praise and glorious worship around the throne of God fill their days. They are eagerly looking forward to Christ's return to earth and the resurrection and transformation of their physical bodies. We know too the angels and all in heaven rejoice when a new believer on earth receives Christ and joins the family of God.

Do you realize how many new believers enter the kingdom statistically every day? Thousands! It's easy to imagine then, the intermediate state as being one long celebration, counting off the days until the last saint is saved and the end of the age is ushered in, and the saints finally receive their new bodies. Perhaps in their spiritual state these saints are already exploring the heavenly city. Perhaps helping Christ prepare for the marriage feast to come and personalizing the individual accommodations within the city. What we are sure of is that they are more fulfilled and more alive than ever before . . . and we will see them again in that glorious city in the sky!

What Will City Life Be Like?

Life with a capital "L" best describes New Jerusalem. As you read the Biblical descriptions of the heavenly city you gain a distinct impression of joyful exuberance. The worship in the throne room is loud and ecstatic and continuous, and we'll talk more of this in the next chapter. Everything is so majestic and glorious there is a deep sense of awe and holiness about city life here.

Living in New Jerusalem in our glorified bodies throughout eternity will be similar to how the saints are already living there, only even more complete and tangible. Besides throne room worship we will enjoy the physical pleasures of living in individually prepared mansions, of exploring the beautiful river garden, the crystal-like lake, and the golden streets. You will enjoy music, art, literature, and all the treasures of the ages in this incredible city.

But it's the relationships in heaven which make this city so exciting to live in. Sure the physical beauty is overwhelming. Just being surrounded with such spectacular opulence, day after day, would be exciting enough. To live together with extended (saved) family, all the Christian friends you've ever known, all the prominent believers you've ever admired in the Bible and history, and Jesus Himself, makes the term "abundant life" take on new significance.

Perfection of beauty is how the Psalmist describes the city of God. The prophets all predict it will be a place of joy and gladness for God's people forever. Glorious things are spoken of this city to come (Psa. 87:3), throughout the Old Testament. Much of what is written about the city of God refers to the re-established city of Jerusalem in the millennial kingdom. However, a careful study of the word Zion, as well as Jerusalem and city of God, reveals the Old Testament writers were also pointing to the eternal city.

The Book of Hebrews in particular helps us see that the Old Testament saints were looking ultimately for a city built by God in the heavens, not just a man-made, restored Jerusalem on this earth. The Old Testament descriptions of this eternal Zion are very similar to the descriptions of New Jerusalem in Revelation. It is seen as a place of beautiful palaces, of peace and love and joy and righteousness. God comes to dwell with His people there forever in the person of the Messiah.

Jesus taught the kingdom of heaven was a present reality for those who would submit to its ruler, as well as their glorious future reward. Paul taught through Christ you can enter the heavenly city now in prayer and praise. The writer of Hebrews says that because of the shed blood of Christ you can come (by faith and in spirit) into the very throne room of God (Heb. 10:19,20).

Thus the New Testament teaches that you can by faith begin heavenly city living now. In Christ, and in your spirit you can begin to experience the excitement, joy, peace, power, fellowship and abundant life of that place where God dwells. Both Testaments speak of material and spiritual blessings to come in this eternal city.

The New Testament highlights the relationships to be enjoyed in the city of God, the fellowship with Christ and with fellow believers. These will indeed be awesome. The focus of our heavenly get-togethers is going to be in the worship center of God's throne room. So let's examine just what these sessions will be like.

CHAPTER 8

HEAVEN'S SEAT OF POWER

What Does the Throne Room in Heaven Look Like?

Ten thousand voices reverberated around the sanctuary. High above the platform a projected, silent movie of the life of Jesus matched the words of the hymn. Five hundred in the choir, two hundred in the orchestra, and every heart focused on Christ. Magnificent harmony, enthusiastic praise, thunderous worship bombarded my hearing, and the balcony shook beneath my feet. My spirit soared and I felt as though the very throne of God would suddenly appear.

If you have ever experienced congregational singing in a huge church where the people genuinely love the Lord, you will know something of what I have just described. Whether or not you like super-churches, worshipping with thousands of others is an experience unlike any other and a very taste of heaven. For most of us the thought of a church seating ten thousand or more is almost too incredible to be believed. But they do exist.

The greatest super-church ever will be in heaven, in the throne room of New Jerusalem. According to John in Revelation, the focal point of the heavenly city is the throne of God. So what is this throne room like and what happens there? The focus of activity is worship of the Lamb. Millions upon millions of saints and angels will lift their voices in magnificent, glorious praise to Him.

Sounds boring? Actually it will be totally awesome and the highlight of our days in heaven. Think back to the last time you attended a major concert (classical or popular) that you really enjoyed, or even to a sporting event (especially if your team won!), or a public celebration of some kind where you were one among thousands. The euphoria of the moment made your flesh tingle and your neck hairs rise. It was almost addictive!

I am not trying to equate worship with entertainment here, God forbid. I am simply reminding you that our gregarious instinct for mass celebration is God given. The most exciting *crowd* moment you have ever experienced is but a taste of what worship in heaven will seem like. True worship in the fellowship of God's people is even closer, and Sunday by Sunday prepares us for the heavenly city.

Color and light and sound fill the throne room of God. From emerald rainbows to the amber glow of fire, from sapphire blue waters to dazzling white robes, from blazing light to dark clouds the scene is amazing. Thunder and lightning, trumpets, choirs, harps and hallelujahs, and God's own voice, deep and loud like the sound of a waterfall.

This is how the Bible describes the throne room of God in heaven. I say throne *room*. Actually it is probably more like a huge, magnificent outdoor temple. The sparkling crystal sea, the waters flowing from the throne to the garden, the atmospheric phenomena, all seem to be an integral part of the Biblical descriptions of God's throne.

Yes, we know from the book of Hebrews much of it is like the temple pattern given to Moses. But when you factor in the millions of angels and worshippers present here, this throne area of the heavenly city must be a kind of super-church worship center beyond description. Actually the whole city is really a temple (worship center) of God (Rev. 21:22).

Once again, I believe, some of what we have already experienced here on earth is a taste of what all this will be like. Have you ever craned your neck in awe at the sweeping columns and intricately carved ceilings of some of Europe's magnificent cathedrals? Have you ever wondered how they must have looked when that stone was brand new and sparkling white and the sanctuary full of people, instead of being dark, dank and empty as so many are now? Then perhaps you've had a glimpse, a taste, of heaven's worship center.

I remember one time in Arkansas visiting a small but beautiful wood and glass chapel in the woods. It was designed so wherever you sat you saw trees and sunlight. The glass went from ceiling to floor so it was hard to tell where the forest ended and the chapel began. It was easy in such a setting to feel at one with creation and the Creator.

I imagine the worship center in heaven to be somewhat like this little chapel, only on a vastly grander scale and surrounded by lakes and rivers and gardens, as well as trees. Any worship place you have visited which has given you a sense of the majesty and awe of God and made you feel like humbly bowing before Him, is I believe a glimpse, a taste of the throne room of heaven. But what of the throne itself?

What Is God's Throne Like?

Rainbows surround the throne of God (Ezek. 1:26-28), green ones according to John (Rev. 4:3). The sky above it is sapphire blue and the floor beneath God's feet is transparent sapphire also. Daniel describes it as a fiery throne set on fiery wheels (Dan. 7:9). The light of God's glory blazes forth from the throne causing most of the Biblical writers who saw it to fall on their faces in awe and fear of God's holiness.

It is obviously made like a seat, a regular throne, for the Lord is always seen to be sitting on it, administering His Holy rule. Once again the earthly images we experience of thrones are a pale pattern of the one in heaven. The thrones of kings and potentates of earth and its history are usually magnificently decorated with gold and rich cloth and precious jewels and raised up so the king can look down on his subjects. So it is in heaven.

Lights, clouds, thunder and lightning, surround God's throne and a spring of pure water wells up from beneath it, flowing out into the river of paradise. In front of the throne is a crystal sea, like glass (Rev. 4:6). Given the crystal river coming out of the throne (Rev. 22:1) this may well be a very calm, mirror-like lake of water. The Tribulation saints are seen standing on this sea of glass singing and playing instruments in praise to God (Rev.15:2). Either they are walking on water, which is entirely possible, or this crystal is some kind of transparent pavement or floor (cf. Exod. 24:10).

Worshippers dominate the throne room of God. Millions of angels and millions of believers sing praises to the Lamb of God on the throne. Actually the scriptures never say angels sing, only speak and cry out. Perhaps only man has the ability to make music with his voice. Music fills the throne room, trumpets, harps and other instruments accompany the worshipping choirs (Rev. 5:9-14; 14:2-3)..

The temple choirs of David and Solomons's reign were huge, skilled and highly organized (1 Chron. 15:16-22). The accompanying orchestras were too. Imagine how vast, magnificent and beautiful the choirs and orchestras of God's tabernacle will be? To be a part of this will be incredible. Even though you think you can't sing or play a note now perhaps one day you will be trained to participate in heaven's music.

Seraphim are the closest individuals to the throne of God. Their task is to praise God continually and apparently to lead everyone else in worship. 24 elders, representing the church, sit close to the throne. They sit on special seats and are dressed in white. The angels stand around the throne and join in the worship of Christ who sits on the throne. White robed martyrs also have a special place near God's throne, they are God's special servants in heaven (Rev.7:14-17).

The four beasts that John describes (Rev. 4:6-9) closely resemble the beasts of Ezekiel's vision of God's throne (Ezek. 1:4-27). Ezekiel identifies these as being Cherubim (Ezek.10). They are half-man, half-beast like creatures with four wings who live continually next to the throne of God. The Seraphim too, worship God day and night around His throne and lead the elders in worship (Rev. 4:9-10).

What Is the Throne Room Used For?

In the throne room are millions of believers from every nation on earth waving banners and praising the Lamb of God on the throne (Rev 7:9-10). It is a place constantly filled with people, with music, voices and light, an exciting place to be. Worship and praise seems to be the primary activity of this part of the heavenly city, where God's throne is. It is the place where God's presence and glory is seen and experienced by everyone in heaven. Here is where the saints and angels alike, communicate with Christ.

What a contrast from the Old Testament where the Shekinah glory of God was seen only once a year on the day of atonement and only by the High Priest. The people were always afraid he wouldn't live to tell the tale, afraid he would never come out again from the Holy of Holies. Even Moses on Mount Sinai was only allowed to see the back (or afterburner) of God's glory (Exod. 33;18-23).

In the New Testament, believers can come boldly before the throne in prayer and faith, but only in the spirit not physically. But then and there in this heavenly city you will all be able to physically enjoy God's presence and glory and talk with Him face to face. Imagine having a daily pass to the Oval Office or Buckingham Palace? Well in this city you get a daily pass and free audience with the King of Kings and Lord of Lords, the Creator of the universe. Wow!

Exhilarating and awesome, perhaps best describe the worship of heaven. John's descriptions especially are of loud, exuberant praise. The angel voices are loud, God's own voice is too, and the sound of instruments playing and people singing. The only time it's recorded there is silence before the throne is when God is about to pour out His final trumpet judgments on earth (Rev.8:1). There won't be any need of judgment again in heaven.

Not that there won't be peace in heaven. He is the God of peace and the Prince of peace. But the throne area seems to be one of perpetual, joyful activity.

Believers are singing old songs and learning new ones (Rev. 5:9; 15:3. Myriad instruments, both string and percussion, accompany this beautiful singing. The angels cry out in praise, the Seraphims too as they lead in worship (Rev. 5:11-14). God's voice booms like the sound of falling water and above it all the elements add their harmony of praise (Rev. 1:15; 4:5).

But all He has to say is "Peace, be still" and I'm sure you could hear a pin drop in the midst of a billion worshippers. What an awesome prospect. We have not yet begun to worship!

Continual praise is offered to God before His throne, led by the seraphim. For the saints it will probably be a daily worship experience as we come to feed on the bread of life, the very words of God Himself and to be refreshed by the water of the Spirit. Given the pattern of the Old Testament worship, there will probably be special worship celebrations as well as remembrance services of what Christ has accomplished.

John records seeing the ark of the covenant, the scriptures, the candlesticks and many of the temple instruments in heaven. Though there is obviously no longer any need for temple sacrifice and ritual, these symbols may well be used to remind us of what Christ has done for us. After all, we will be in heaven only because of His great love and sacrifice. I am sure the worship services in heaven will be creative and progressive, incredibly moving and beautiful, and never boring.

Translation into the city from the new earth or anywhere else in the new universe will get you instantly into the throne room and the presence of God. It can obviously be physically accessed from within the city itself. Prayer or a similar kind of spiritual communication will enable the believer to communicate with Christ at any time from anywhere in heaven. There will never be a busy signal!

Though the Bible does not specify where the throne is inside the city it most certainly will be either in the center or at the apex. The tabernacle in the wilderness was always pitched in the center of the camp, with the children of Israel's tents all around it. The temple was built in the northern corner of the highest part of Jerusalem. Either way God's throne is high and lifted up and the focal point of New Jerusalem.

High and holy is God's throne according to the Old Testament prophets. It is a throne of glory, justice and judgment, the place where God sits surrounded by the hosts (angels) of heaven. Ezekiel predicts that God's throne will be the place where He will one day live with His children forever (Ezek.43:7).

The 70 elders that went up Mount Sinai with Moses saw the throne of God (Exod.24:10). Their description of its sapphire-like transparent walls is very similar to Isaiah, Ezekiel and John's visions of heaven. The Psalmist speaks of God's throne being in His Holy temple in heaven, once again in a similar way to John's description.

In fact most of the Book of Revelation is Old Testament imagery. It is impossible to fully understand it without a knowledge of the Old Testament. John, through the Holy Spirit, simply expands on what God had already revealed to the prophets. The clouds and atmosphere around the throne, the colors, the light, the sounds, the general appearance, and the predictions of the Messiah one day sitting on this throne are all from the Old Testament.

Christ is the New Testament focus of the throne of God. John sees the glorified Savior sitting on the throne of God judging the churches, judging the earth, judging the devil and his demons, judging mankind and ruling forever with His saints. But for the believer this throne becomes a throne of grace, not judgment (Heb. 4:16).

Presently Christ sits at the right hand of God the Father interceding for His children on earth. Your prayers go to the throne room of God, administered by the seraphim and the twenty four church elders (Rev. 5:8). Ephesians teaches through faith and prayer believers can spiritually sit with Christ now in this throne room of grace (Eph. 2:6).

In the future, in heaven, every knee will bow before Christ on the throne, acknowledging Him as Lord. The nations will bring their cultural gifts to Him at that throne room in the heavenly city. Jesus will rule the new universe from this throne.

Why Is There A Garden There?

Life began in a garden for mankind and there is therefore a garden near the throne room in heaven, the garden of God . . . paradise. Just as God walked with Adam in Eden so He will walk with us in heaven's garden. Water is essential to life and the source of all water comes from the throne in the form of a river that flows through the garden. The water also represents the life giving power of the Holy Spirit.

As you read John's account of this garden (Rev. 22:1-5), you get the impression the throne area is in the middle of this garden. What a beautiful contrast to the exuberant noise and activity of the worship around the throne, to then stroll the quiet streets and river banks of paradise. Heaven is so full of unexpected, wonderful contrasts, I know I am going to love living there.

Trees of Life cover the banks of this river. Remember the tree of Life in the garden of Eden? The fruit of these trees sustain life forever also. The nations of the new earth come and eat of them so the garden will always have people strolling through it. But of course, like everything else in this vast heavenly city, this magnificent garden will be huge, probably more like a whole garden State than a private backyard.

There will be no more thorns or weeds or fierce animals here, only peace and light and incredible natural beauty. The river will be full of fish, according to Ezekiel's vision (Ezek. 47:1-12), and the trees will bare fruit every month. Notice how closely John's account in Revelation mirrors the Old Testament imagery of Ezekiel. Sure, Ezekiel was prophesying about more immediate events in Israel, but he was also pointing to the eternal temple of God in eternity. What an awesome place this is going to be to explore. You've never been to a resort quite like this!

Beyond the sky, beyond the stars God rules now from His throne in heaven. It is part of His Holy temple or tabernacle (Psa. 11:4), and is therefore now part of the heavenly city, the New Jerusalem home Christ has prepared for His saints. At present the throne of God is right here, on a spiritual plane accessed by prayer and faith.

Even back in Exodus, Moses and the 70 elders were able to physically see God's throne from earth. The New Testament teaches it is only a prayer or praise away. Think about this for a moment. If you are a child of His then every time you pray, you are transported spiritually to that very throne (Eph. 2:6). You can, as it were, enter heaven now and have an audience with the King of Kings.

So why can't I see it now? Probably because we are not as spiritually discerning as Elisha was (2 Kings 6:16-17). Or perhaps we would, like the apostle Paul was tempted to do (2 Cor. 12:7), become proud of our spiritual vision and begin to worship the physical experience of the throne rather than the One on the throne.

What Does God Do from His Throne?

Power flows from the throne of God. He has chosen to control the world from here. As the prophets predict God will one day live among and fellowship with his people from here. As in the past so more so in eternity God chooses to bless the earth and His children from His throne in heaven.

At present God judges the world from His throne. He controls the weather and the seasons and the politics of earth from here. It is from His throne that He hears the prayers of His people, forgives, admonishes, blesses and supports them. It is from this throne of grace He calls to lost mankind, longing to restore fellowship with all of His children.

God looks down from this sanctuary (holy place) in heaven to watch over the affairs of earth (Psa. 102: 19). He speaks to men's hearts from here, answering their prayers and supplying their need. He demonstrates His judgment and His glory, visibly on earth from the throne. Mercy and truth proceed from His throne. God sent His Son to earth from here to redeem mankind. What an incredible place this throne of God is. One day you will stand before it. You will see God face to face . . . and live!

But what of the practical wonders of heaven? What will I look like when I visit the throne room? What will I feel like? What will I do in heaven? How will I pass the time?

PART III.

A NEW LIFE

CHAPTER 9

WHAT WILL I LOOK LIKE?

What Kind of Body Will I Have in Heaven?

"Orienteering" they called it, with 50-pound packs on our backs, a compass, one topographical map and three days to find our way back to base camp. The instructors had dropped us in the middle of nowhere. We'd never make it. The mountains seemed too high, the rivers too wide and the distances impossible. But the previous few weeks of intensive physical training back at the Outward Bound School paid off. Much to our own surprise, all but one of us made it back safely and on time.

The daily routine of being made to stretch yourself to your own limits and beyond, had rapidly hardened our bodies and our resolve. I have never been so fit in all my life the day I graduated from that summer course. It felt terrific. Back in high school (I was only fifteen), for the first few games of the rugby season I ran rings around the opposition and scored more tries (touch downs) than I ever had before. I felt like I could outrun a cheetah! I felt like I'd gained a new body.

What an incredible feeling to be so fit and healthy. Why can't we stay like that all our lives? In heaven we will! The Bible promises us we will indeed gain new bodies. They will be strong and healthy like Jesus' glorious risen body, never to suffer sickness, hurt or the aches of old age. Never again will you experience that Monday morning feeling where you can barely drag your weary body out of bed. Every day in heaven will feel like the first day of vacation. Every day you will be physically and spiritually "pumped" to get on with living for the Lord. There'll be so many exciting things to do and look forward to.

What a fantastic future life is in store for those who love Christ. Man, I can't wait to be there! How about you? But isn't all this just wishful thinking, pie in the sky? Please read and meditate on 1 Corinthians chapter 15 and see what God says through the apostle Paul about the resurrection and our new bodies.

How do we know what our new bodies will be like? Because Jesus came back from the dead in a new body and was seen by hundreds of eye witnesses. He has shown us what is to come. As Paul says, if Jesus didn't rise from the dead then our faith is in vain. But He did and has become the firstfruits, or forerunner or example of what will happen to all those dead bodies of the saints currently decaying in the grave (1 Cor. 17-23).

Immortal bodies, no longer subject to decay and corruption of any kind, that's what our new bodies will be like . . . perfect in every way. Even a today's Mr. Universe would be considered a weakling compared to the strength of an angel. In heaven all of us will be even more powerful than the angels. We will be like Christ. Everything about our physical form will be controlled by the spirit. In that sense we will have spiritual bodies in heaven (1 Cor. 15:44).

We marvel at those who through mental toughness can make their (mortal) bodies endure intense pain or achieve incredible feats of endurance and skill. Every athlete knows the importance of mind over matter in terms of controlling what can be achieved by our bodies. Under the pressure of intense competition many super-sports-stars speak of reaching another skill level where their bodies are almost on automatic pilot achieving things even they thought impossible.

Imagine if (when!) our perfect, immortal physical bodies are totally controlled by our perfect spirits, overriding the mind and emotions? What incredible achievements we will make in heaven! Wouldn't you love to have a body like this?

Peter was able to walk on water, with Jesus' help, even in his mortal body. John saw the saints standing on the crystal sea in heaven. If by faith we can move mountains and walk on water now, just imagine the power we will have in heaven. There'll still be physical laws in operation. But, like Christ, we'll have the ability to override them when necessary.

Yes, I believe we will be able to do all the things Jesus did physically while on earth including controlling the weather. Our motivation, of course, for exercising this power will be to glorify God not for selfish satisfaction. We will have incredibly different bodies in terms of ability and spiritual control yet very similar in general appearance.

So What Will I Look Like?

The women and the disciples all recognized Jesus after the resurrection. I know they couldn't believe it was Him until he spoke to them, and the Emmaus road disciples were kept from recognizing Him at first. Of course, dear old Thomas refused to believe his senses until he saw the nail-print scars. Nevertheless Jesus must have looked very similar to what they had become used to. We will too in heaven.

But what if I'm not happy with the way I look now? You are already beautiful in God's eyes. He doesn't create mistakes. What we call imperfections are really special opportunities to highlight God's grace to us and through us. Yes, you'll get a new, perfect body but you will still be uniquely you!

Jesus, while on earth, was nothing special to look at the Bible tells us (Isa. 53:2). Though He was immensely fit and strong, for He endured hard labor (carpentry), forty days without food, hundreds of miles of walking, and excruciating punishment from the Romans. But it was the attractiveness of His personality which drew all men to Him. His meekness (strength under control), made Him unique as a person and a leader. You will be like Him.

So you needn't be upset if you feel you don't come up to Hollywood or Madison Avenue standards of attractiveness. Praise God for the beautiful people but without the inner peace of God those stars and models will deteriorate soon enough. Does this mean I won't be very attractive in heaven? Of course not. There are no ugly people in God's family. In heaven you will look and feel like a star (Dan. 12:3).

It's just our society is so image conscious and our idea of what is attractive so conditioned by Hollywood, sex, and the media we've forgotten about the power of inner beauty. In your new body you may well look like someone in their thirties in the prime of life and health. This is what Jesus was when He died and rose again, and we will have new bodies just like His, the Bible says. Believe me, you will be absolutely glowing with physical and spiritual strength and vitality, brighter and more attractive than you've ever been in your life! Forever young! What a hope, what a reality to come!

Remember, your physical body is just the temple, the frame if you like around the true picture of who you really are, your spirit and personality. In heaven they will be Christ-like. His resurrected body retained the scars of the nail-prints, so there may be some unique "leftovers" from the past that reflect the glory of God in your life. But there will be no deformities or physical abnormalities. You will be perfect and glorified just like Jesus, even in your thoughts.

What about My Mind, Emotions, and Spirit?

Truth is found ultimately in Jesus Christ. He is the way the truth and the life. Yet even for believers whose minds are being transformed into the mind of Christ, we still see as in an unpolished mirror, says Paul (1 Cor. 13:12). In heaven, we will know as we are known by God. We will understand ourselves and the purpose of our life from His perspective. Does this mean we will know everything in heaven? No, we will spend eternity learning more and more about God, and therefore about everything that is.

How do I know this? Because Jesus defines eternal life as *knowing* God (John 17:3). Yet the Scriptures also say God is beyond finding out (else He wouldn't really be God) (Job. 11:7; Rom. 11:3). Part of the fun of eternity will be learning more and more about God and His glory, and discovering the marvels of His creation. The difference will be that in our glorified, spirit-controlled bodies and minds, we will be able to fully understand, appreciate and appropriate, the things we learn.

92

Our discoveries in heaven will not be hampered by intellectual pride or ignorance. They will always be in the light of truth. We will touch on this further when we talk about the activities of heaven. Suffice to say that nobody will suffer from Alzheimer's disease in heaven and yes, you will be able to finally understand algebra, if you want to!

Holiness is the essence of God. Without holiness no one can see God. This is why Paul describes our new bodies as being spiritual and heavenly, as opposed to being natural or fleshly (1 Cor. 15:44-50). Through the atoning blood of Christ we (all believers) have been washed clean and made spiritually holy in the sight of God the Father. In heaven we will be physically holy also.

This promise of Scripture is truly awesome and a little hard to grasp from our present earthbound view. Like Jesus after the resurrection we will become both physical and spiritual beings. He walked through closed doors, traveled huge distances instantly, still performed miracles over nature, yet physically enjoyed fish and chips on the beach with his friends (John 21:9-14)! He ascended through the clouds into heaven.

God is spirit yet with a permanent physical form in the person of Jesus. We are made in God's image and one day we will be like Him (Jesus). Though the angels can appear in human form (Gen. 18:2; 19:1, 5), they do not have a permanent physical body. They were created as spiritual beings with a beautiful but spirit form only. In our new permanent, physical bodies we will be able to utilize both realms, the spiritual and the physical, just like Jesus.

Amazing! Incredible! Truth is indeed stranger than fiction. Star Wars doesn't even come close to the real thing. God is much, much more than a force, the source of ultimate power, He is a living person. As such he is intimately concerned with His creation and longs for eternal fellowship with the persons He has made in His own image.

God, therefore, has personality, mind, will and emotions just like He has made us. In heaven you will still experience emotions. The difference will be instead of self-centered depression, sadness, anger, hate and fear, there will be Christ-centered love, joy, peace, patience and all the fruit of the spirit (Gal. 5:22-23). Your soul (mind, will and emotions) will come under the complete domination of the spirit.

Even now, the spiritual drive in man is actually the strongest drive we have. It's just that our sin natures deny it and we become totally controlled by our senses and feelings. Which is why you will never find satisfaction and fulfillment without God. Only He can rebirth your spirit again. Religion can't do it, only a personal relationship with a personal God, Jesus. In heaven you will be finally fulfilled as a person, spiritually, physically, emotionally, consciously (there will be no sub-conscious).

How Will I Be Known in Heaven?

Names are very important in the Bible. They not only identify the individual but frequently signify what God has planned for their lives. This is why God often changed names in response to faith, such as Abram to Abraham. In heaven you will be given new names. The most significant of these names will be presented to you engraved on a special white stone (Rev. 2:17).

The new name written on it is presently known only to Christ and will probably signify the unique work He has done within you while you were on earth. It will typify your (Christ-like) personality. In heaven we will not be robot-like clones. Each person will retain their uniqueness and distinctiveness summed up in their new name.

I believe that we will also have a common "family-of-God" surname. A name of God is written or implanted on the forehead of each saint in heaven (Rev. 3:17; 14:1). This name is described as being the name of God *and* the name of the city of God, New Jerusalem. The Messiah was to be called "the Lord our righteousness" (Jer. 23:6). Jeremiah also prophesied that the future city of God, (new) Jerusalem was to be called "the Lord our righteousness" (Jer. 33:16)!

In heaven, therefore, every time this surname (Jehovah-*tsidkenu*) is recorded or spoken, or someone is called by their full name, we will be reminded of the only reason we are in heaven . . . the Lord our righteousness. So if we get new names in heaven do we also get new clothes? Whatever do they dress like in heaven?

City-wear for New Jerusalem, at least within the throne-room limits, appears to be exclusively white. The redeemed, like Christ, wear white linen robes with gold accessories whenever in His presence (Rev.4:4; 7:9; 19:8, 14). On the new earth I am sure we will wear much more varied and colorful attire, perhaps reflecting our cultural glories. Since the new earth seems to be the place where we will engage in creative work and ruling authority, we may well have special work clothes or even uniforms to wear there.

Given the detailed intricacy, color, style and beauty of the Old Testament priestly vestments prescribed by God (Exod. 28:4-43), the clothing of new earth will gloriously reflect the beauty of Christ and His creation. Just imagine the creativity of a fashion industry that was not governed by profit or sensuality?

Saints will be the only kind of people in heaven. Not specially "good" people, just those who have put their faith in Christ's righteousness instead of their own. They will come from every culture, race and color under the sun (Rev. 7:9). Loved ones and extended family members who have trusted Christ alone for salvation will greet you when you arrive.

It is interesting to note when God calls His saints home in the Bible how often He describes it to them as being "gathered unto *thy people*" (Num. 20:24; 27:13). Clearly your immediate family relationships continue in heaven even though you will be closely related to everyone in the family of God. Your loved ones will still be special to you there.

Those with few close relatives on earth will discover they are related to many new "loved ones" in heaven. God is a father to the fatherless (Psa. 68:5). He longs to communicate love to His children.

What Language Will We Speak?

Prayer has always been the primary spiritual communication between mankind and heaven. As spiritually controlled beings in eternity, prayer will continue to be a means of communicating with the Lord, if not with others. Throughout scripture God has also communicated verbally, and in writing to men. Ancient Hebrew may well be the spoken language of heaven, given that it is the language of God's people Israel, the Ten Commandments, and the only language specifically mentioned as being spoken from heaven (Acts 26:14).

During the millennial reign of Christ on this earth we know there will be a universal language (Zeph. 3:9). This may well be the language of eternity. Jesus, of course, spoke Greek and Aramaic, and obviously knew Hebrew. Given the continuance of national distinctiveness in heaven, and the beauty of many individual languages, there may well be a multitude of languages preserved on the new earth but with one official language, for God is the God of order not confusion.

Remember the Holy Spirit was able to instantly interpret languages and dialects for the people at Pentecost and enabled the apostles to speak them. So it won't be a barrier for those of you who find it hard enough to understand even your own language!

Communication through the written word is very much a part of heaven, from the Bible itself to the detailed records and official documents that John saw being read and proclaimed in heaven. Whether computers or some other advanced system is used in heaven is immaterial at this point. There will be libraries kept of past material and yet-to-come records. For a bookworm like myself this would be heaven just to spend a day in one of the New Jerusalem libraries.

When we are not visiting libraries or singing in the throne room we will probably be feasting, and we'll talk of this more under activities and relationships. The question then arises as to whether our new, immortal bodies will even need food?

Will I Eat in Heaven?

Fruit trees line the river in paradise and these trees are trees of *life* (Rev. 22:2). They bear different fruit each month, all year round. The leaves of the trees are also for our health and well being. Clearly then the fruit is for our enjoyment and for our eternal sustenance.

Does this mean we will die if we don't eat of the tree of life? Well, that's a bit like asking; will I die if I refuse to take another breath? Technically, yes, but no one in their right mind refuses to breathe. Even if you are crazy enough to try and force yourself to stop breathing you'll soon become unconscious, and so automatically resume breathing. What I am saying is the question is mute.

The Bible indicates in heaven you will partake of the tree of life to sustain eternal life in your physical body. It also says that you will partake of the bread of life (Christ and His word to us), and of the water of life (the Holy Spirit) to sustain your spiritual life. Of course you will also drink of the pure, physical water for your physical body. Remember too, you will be perfect then, always desiring to do the will of God, and unable to sin or disobey.

The exciting thing is heaven is full of feasts and feasting. Starting with the marriage feast of the Lamb and continuing with family celebrations and feast days throughout eternity. As already mentioned, Jesus enjoyed breakfast (and earthly food) with the disciples in His resurrection body. These things in Scripture indicate we will be able to enjoy a variety of culinary delights, both in New Jerusalem and on the new earth. Of course, like Adam and Eve before the Fall, no animals will be slaughtered for food. But best of all we can eat just for enjoyment, and not have to worry about gaining weight or ever getting sick. Why would anyone not want to go to heaven?

I guess this last response just shows my fleshly appetite (pun intended)! Speaking of physical appetites, whenever we talk about our glorified bodies the question is always asked, "Will there be sex in heaven?"

Will There Be Sex in Heaven?

Angels, Jesus taught, do not marry (Matt.22:30). They do not, therefore, have sexual relationships or produce children. We will be like them in this aspect in heaven, Jesus said. Actually, angels in the Bible, by name and appearance, are only recorded as being male. God created us male and female in His image. I know Paul says there is neither male nor female in Christ (Gal. 3:28). But he is talking about equality and importance between the sexes. Adam was incomplete without Eve. Man and woman together uniquely reflect the fullness of God. We will retain our gender in Heaven (just as Jesus did after the resurrection), but the joy of physical sex will somehow be replaced by the joy of spiritual intimacy.

Believe me, it will be better than sex and I am not being irreverent saying this. The God who gave us the wonder, excitement, fulfillment and ecstasy of physical union within marriage is more than able to replace and exceed the joy of this gift in heaven. Since there is no procreation in heaven, our glorified new bodies may not need the same hormonal drives, anyway. Yes, sex is a very powerful drive now, but despite what our current pop culture would have us believe, the spiritual drive in man is really the one which longs most to be satisfied.

Go travel the globe or read up on world history, and you'll find it is the spiritual belief systems that drive and define the culture of people and nations. We are all spiritual creatures (not just physical and sexual), desperately searching for meaning to our lives, desperately searching for God.

Sex within marriage is an immediate expression of the oneness God intends for all marriages. Becoming one in mind and spirit, as well as body, is an even deeper expression of that oneness. It brings a more lasting joy and satisfaction than sex alone ever could. But spiritual intimacy takes time and unselfish commitment and few couples seem to achieve it. It is a taste of heaven.

Though Jesus taught there will be no marriages in heaven, I do believe from other principles in Scripture that special relationships on earth will continue to be special in heaven. You will get to spend all the time you want to with your earthly spouse (or spouses?). If there are no marriages in heaven, beyond the marriage feast of the Lamb, and no sex, then does this mean there will be no children in heaven?

Adam was created an adult, so was Eve. Which answers the familiar chicken and egg question. Which came first? According to the Bible the chicken came first. Adam was made complete, mature and highly intelligent. He did not start out as a child nor evolve from some ape form (Gen. 2:7). In heaven everything is perfect and complete. No one will be immature (1 Cor. 13: 10-11). God's goal for our lives now is to become "grown up" believers

(Heb. 5:12-14), perfect as He is perfect (Matt. 5:48). It appears therefore, there can be no children in heaven, though we will all be adult "children" of our heavenly Father.

So what happens to children that die now? They will become mature adults in heaven. So how will you recognize them? You'll know. Many a parent has met up with missing, adopted, believed dead children when they were adults and instinctively knew they were theirs.

"My, look how you've grown" is going to echo all round the heavenly city!

But I love children, you protest. How can it be heaven without them? In heaven God will more than fulfill that natural instinct with a new love toward everyone, especially our "spiritual" children and immediate families. We will love one another as children and like a child, in absolute faith and trust (Matt. 18:3-4). After all, what forty, fifty or even eighty year old hasn't felt like a child inside, despite their outward age? So we already have a taste of what Kingdom living will be like. Let's face it, it's not the crying, the helplessness, the messes, the immaturity of children that we love. It's the unfeigned joy of life, the exuberance, the inquisitiveness, the laughter, the spontaneous affection. In heaven we will all be like that!

What about the Handicapped?

Unblemished physical wholeness was required for service in the Priesthood. There could be no lameness, blindness, crookedness, missing limbs or even a broken nose (Lev. 21:16-24). As with everything else about tabernacle worship, nothing could mar the picture of God's perfect holiness. In heaven not only will everything and everyone be physically perfect in order to live with a holy God but there will also be no more pain or sorrow or physical discomfort of any kind.

The deaf, the dumb, the blind, the lame, will all be healed and in perfect health in heaven. There will be no "handicaps," physical or mental. All will be whole and holy. What a wonderful hope heaven gives us. But if everyone is strong and healthy, has an endless supply of food and drink, and material wealth beyond their dreams, what on earth will we do in heaven? Won't we get bored living forever and ever. Will we work in heaven or what?

CHAPTER 10

WHAT WILL I DO FOREVER AND EVER?

Will I Be Bored in Heaven?

Vacations are a huge industry today, especially in my home State. Living in sunny Florida I feel like I am on vacation all the time. Why? Because I lie around on the beaches all day? No! Because I am doing what I love, surrounded by people I love, in an incredibly beautiful part of the USA that I love, and I have opportunity to reach out in love to others.

That's why heaven will never be boring. You will work at what you love doing together with people who love you, all for the Glory of God. It won't seem like work at all. The environment, our homes, the weather, the achievements, the rewards, the satisfaction will not just be beautiful, they will be perfect!

"Are we there yet?" "What are we going to do for a whole week?" "Is there a swimming pool?" "How much can I spend?" "What do we do if it rains?" "Will you take me to . . . ?"

Family vacations can be fun and the time goes by so fast, and so does the money. We usually promise ourselves that we'll rest, relax and take it easy this time but it rarely happens. It's doing new things and seeing new places which makes a holiday exciting and different from the humdrum of the weekly grind. There's nothing more boring than being in a hotel room, or even on a beach, when there's nothing new to do or see, no more money left to spend, and no one to talk to.

Fellowship with others is an important part of the activities in heaven. Fellowship with God is the primary activity, highlighted by daily praise and worship in the throne room of the heavenly city. What a glorious, exciting way to be emotionally, spiritually and physically primed for the daily work projects Christ assigns us.

It will be as exciting as planning what to do and where to go on the first morning of vacation. The throne room is where we daily receive the spiritual food and drink necessary for eternal life. It is the center of all activity in heaven, both on the new earth and in New Jerusalem.

There will be so much to see and do in the throne room you will never want to miss these sessions. First and foremost you get to see Jesus. Then there are angels to talk to, friends and famous people to meet, songs to learn, music to be practiced, a joyful worship service to participate in, and the glory of God to admire in all His light, beauty, color and sound.

What a glorious start to the day, in the palace of the King. It goes on forever and ever. You will never tire of it or be bored by it. It will be the focus of your life. But what else will you do when you are not singing in the sanctuary of heaven?

Feasting is very much a part of heaven. In fact the first major event in eternity will be a wedding feast (Rev. 19:7,9). Visiting and fellowshipping with the millions of saints as well as with our immediate families will occupy much of our time in eternity.

The Bible paints a picture of heaven that involves sitting and dining together. God comes in and eats with us (Rev. 3:20). Jesus promised His disciples He would drink again with them again in the kingdom (Matt. 26:29). The prophets saw God's people eating together in families on their own land. The Levitical feasts of Israel are spiritually fulfilled in the Messiah and there was no further need for sacrificial offerings once He had come. Yet every one of these feasts were to be kept by the children of Israel, *forever* (Lev. 23:41).

Given the altar, and the temple vessels John sees being used in heaven it is entirely probable many of the Old Testament feasts (minus the meat) will continue to be celebrated in heaven forever, in joyful remembrance of what Christ has accomplished. They will be transformed into great, festive, family feasts, thankful anniversaries of the goodness of God.

If you have ever experienced a family reunion dinner, where several generations are present and people arrive from all over the country you haven't met for years, you've already had a taste of heaven (assuming, of course, your family gets along!) In heaven every one will get along, in fact they will be ecstatic to see you.

Will We Work in Heaven?

Serving Christ and others will be a large part of the work you will do in heaven. Jesus taught the greatest people in heaven will be those who were the greatest servants on earth. You will serve Him by helping Him rule His kingdom, especially on the new earth. Then, too, as part of glorifying Christ forever, you will use and develop your God-given creativity in the particular areas He assigns you.

Using your creative talents for the glory of God will not seem like work at all. Think of the things you love to work at today, the things you are good at, the things which give you a deep sense of satisfaction when you complete them. This is what work in heaven will be like. Remember work was not part of the curse of sin. Adam worked the garden and took care of the animals before the fall. It was the struggle of working just to survive, with all the hindrances of sin natures in a fallen, corrupted, decaying world that made work a curse for man.

Perhaps you can't think of any kind of work you really love doing that will be in heaven. I am sure the Lord already has something very special planned, just for you.

Imagine a working environment free from the restrictions of time, money, selfishness, greed, sickness, tiredness, laziness, pain, frustration and even mistakes. How incredibly satisfying and rewarding work will be in heaven, doing what you love doing with people who love you and all for the glory of God.

Discovering all there is to know about creation and the new universe will be part of your responsibilities in heaven. Just as it was in the beginning when man was given dominion over creation. He was to subdue the earth, name and organize the animal kingdom and cultivate the garden for the glory of God and his own well-being.

Each of us will have some familial, local responsibilities as we joyfully live together in family units. Exactly how God will make up those family units is not clear and of course we won't be limited to them or by them for we will be one big family of God. But the picture the prophets and Psalmists paint of eternity, and the context of words such as *joy* and *everlasting* give an impression of celebrating, feasting, homes and loved ones. Indeed the church itself is to teach us how to love as *family* those who are strangers to us, to remind us in Christ we are all brothers and sisters.

Marriage and the family unit was the first institution created by God as a reflection of the oneness of the triune Godhead. In heaven, family gatherings will continue to do just this.

The spiritual leaders in heaven, will be given the highest responsibility and authority under Christ. The Patriarchs, too will be especially honored there. John saw *elders*, spiritual leaders representing the church in the throne room. Many will be given political responsibility as kings, presidents and rulers over nations and cities. But best of all will be the fact all of our *bosses* in heaven will also be the humblest of individuals and therefore a joy to serve under.

In the Old Testament Israel was not content with a pure Theocracy, they wanted a king to rule over them. Even when God gave them a king the final authority for God's people was not the monarch or the judges but the prophet, the one with the word of God. Christ, the king of kings, and great high priest, will of course hold absolute and final authority in heaven. In the day to day running and ruling of the nations, those who know and understand His word, the spiritual leaders, will guide and direct all other authority.

There will be no incompetent, unspiritual or arrogant leaders in Christ's kingdom. The creative assignments Christ gives you will be supervised by the best bosses you have ever worked for. They will strive to serve *you*, even as you serve those under you so everyone is happy in their work and together bring glory to Christ. Wow! How soon can I submit an application? Utopia on earth!

Except this utopia is theocratic (God ruled), not socialistic or even democratic. Christ is Lord and He is the one we work for.

Will I Learn New Skills in Heaven?

Glorifying God in all you do will be much easier in heaven given all of the skilled *experts* available to talk to and help you. The gifts and abilities Christ has helped you develop on earth will continue to progress in heaven and be used to teach others. Just because you will be perfect does not mean you will instantly and automatically know everything or be able to do anything and everything perfectly (else you would be God!).

Part of the joy of heaven will be learning new skills to the glory of God. Have you ever wanted to write a symphony? Imagine studying under Beethoven? Have you longed to paint like a Rembrandt, sculpt like a Michael Angelo, play piano like a Chopin, calculate like an Einstein, invent things like a Thomas Edison or design buildings like a Frank Lloyd Wright? Assuming any of these characters are in heaven, you'll get to spend as much time with them as you want.

Think of all the skilled, gifted stars you admire, past or present, you would love to emulate. If their talent is one which brings glory to God and they are true believers who will be in heaven, then you will get to meet them and learn from them as much as you like. And it won't cost you a dime.

Art and the arts in general are mankind's response to the glory of God all around him. In his pride, selfishness and sensuality man often distorts this glory but in heaven the arts will flourish, pure and beautiful, forever reflecting the majesty of the Creator. The new earth will be where we create and build and perform beautiful things for Christ. The nations will bring the best of their cultural creative works to New Jerusalem (Rev. 21:24).

The physical, creative work you engage in on the new earth will be your worship when you are not actively singing His praises in the heavenly city's throne room. Just as the Scripture tell us that the natural world declares the glory of God (Psa. 19:1), so in heaven the artistic, creative skills of man will continually declare His glory also.

105

Think of how much a beautiful piece of music or art, a book or a poem, even a magnificent building or some human physical skill can bring a sense of wonder, peace and joy to our souls. In heaven *everything* you see, hear, touch or do will cause you to thank God and give you an overwhelming sense of fulfillment and contentment.

Records of the past and present are kept in heaven now. The Bible itself is preserved in heaven. There will be books of some kind there and we will continue to learn about God, about creation, about the universe. Yes, you will still be learning new things in heaven. Remember, you will have all the experts to call on whenever you don't fully understand or can't accomplish what you want to. They will lovingly and patiently impart to you all that Christ has taught them.

So, yes, you will read and study and listen and learn in heaven but it will never become a chore. Some of you are probably thinking, "What if I don't like to read and study?" Don't worry, I'm sure there will be all kinds of heavenly holographs or "ultimate reality" multi-media presentations for you to watch instead! It will be easy to learn in Christ's kingdom and we will have all the time in the world. I can think of a few skills I lack now that may take me forever to learn! But it will all be fun. At His right hand are pleasures forever more.

Eden was an uncultivated garden that Adam had to take care of and creatively beautify. Vineyards and cornfields are seen by the prophets to be in heaven. Domestic, work animals as well as (former) wild animals are there. We will plant and cultivate and grow things on the new earth, just like Adam, to beautify it even more to the glory of God.

Personally I have somewhat of a brown thumb especially when it comes to house plants, yet I love flowers and gardens. In heaven I can learn from master gardeners and growers and be able to beautify whatever land the Lord assigns me on the new earth.

Have you ever spent a day in your garden, weeding, planting, watering, clipping, nurturing and even talking to your plants? It can be backbreaking work but somehow worth it all when you see the flowers blooming, and smell their fragrances and marvel at the color and delicate magnificence of it all. There will be no thorns or obnoxious weeds in heaven! So it will never seem like work.

Will There Be Leisure Time in Heaven?

Relationships, maintaining and improving the ones we have and developing new ones, will take up a large part of our time in heaven. We tend to put off spending the time we should on relationships today in favor of more urgent (we assume), physical tasks. Heaven is defined as rest, not so much from work but from the worries and pressures of work that we have become so used to in a fallen world today. In heaven there will be plenty of time for celebration, relaxation and simply "chewing the fat" with others.

You will never feel guilty at taking time off to talk with others or listen to the Lord, as Martha did (Luke 10:39-42). Yes, there will be leisure time in heaven in the sense of not having to work constantly at physical tasks. Time to enjoy the presence of God, the magnificence of His creation, the joy of close friendships, the excitement of another's talent and creative gift. All of these things will bless your days in heaven.

Celebration, holy days (holidays) of fellowshipping and feasting together is a vibrant part of heaven. It is very much associated with *joy* and *rejoicing* in the Bible. Food, conversation, singing, shouting, praise, nature, music, thankfulness, rewards, prayer and people, are all associated with *rejoicing* in heaven. This is how we will celebrate together. The feasts of the Old Testament went on for days. Imagine how long the parties in heaven will last!

We will have material rewards to celebrate and enjoy too, Jesus taught, and we will willingly share them with everyone. There will be special feast days to remember and thank Christ for all he has done for us.

Many of the family events we naturally celebrate and rejoice over now are but a taste of life in heaven. Accomplishment of tasks, excellence of service, the glory of creative skills diligently performed, will all receive communal acknowledgment and celebration. Nothing worthwhile will go unnoticed. You'll never suffer poor self-esteem in heaven! It will be a time (an eternity) of great joy and satisfaction in everything you do.

All the glory will be given to Christ. But won't that take away personal satisfaction? No more than an Oscar winner who humbly acknowledges they couldn't have achieved success without the help of others.

Laughter is good for body and soul (Prov. 15:13,15; 17:22). It will be very much a part of life in heaven. Those with a gift of making others laugh will enrich us all if not formally entertain us. I doubt if there will be Hollywood style movie entertainment in heaven (after all heaven is real and eternal not make believe) but we may be able to enjoy watching earth's past history through some kind of spiritual time travel or "ultimate reality" recordings. On second thoughts, creative drama can indeed bring glory to God when it reflects the beauty and uniqueness of human relationships. So all you actors out there take hope.

There is so much to see, do, experience and explore in heaven it seems there will be no need of organized entertainment. I guess it depends on how you define the word *entertainment*. If you take entertainment's primary meaning, hospitality, then there will be plenty of this going on in heaven. In addition there will be museums, libraries, cultural displays, and exhibitions of creative talent to visit.

Music, of course, plays a prominent part in eternity. Besides the awesome choirs and orchestras of the worship center in New Jerusalem the new earth will have its musical centers too. All music is supposed to bring glory to God. The musical talent in heaven will be vast, varied and incredibly beautiful to listen to.

Whether it is under the stars or in some magnificent city building on the new earth or in New Jerusalem itself we will, I am sure, get to spend endless hours of enjoying spirit-soaring music. If you have never learned music appreciation on earth, you will certainly do so in heaven. It will bless your soul.

Recreation that is pure and unselfish can be honoring to God too. It can develop relationships, an appreciation for God-given skills, an opportunity for humility, a chance to work as a team, an enjoyment of creation, and gratitude for being healthy and alive. So will there be golf courses, team sports, and other such forms of entertainment in heaven? The Bible doesn't really answer this one.

We can only surmise from Biblical principles, namely, anything we enjoy in this life that honors God, His people, His creation, is a taste of what will be in heaven. Though time will be endless we will not waste time there. Anything that develops relationships, of course, is never a waste of time in God's eyes.

I hope I can finally learn to hit a golf ball straight, in heaven. I love walking (why do they have to speed things up with carts today?) beautiful green fairways, as much to enjoy the magnificence of creation as to play golf. I have also developed and deepened many a relationship between swings. So I hope the Lord will let us build a few courses on the new earth but if He doesn't I am sure I'll be too busy and happy doing something else to ever miss it. Remember there will be no regrets or sorrow in heaven.

If there are sports activities in heaven, will I get brand new custom fit gear? Will I get to own some of the "toys" I never had here? Will there be any material ownership in heaven? Will it mean as much to us as it apparently does here? What rewards await me in heaven?

CHAPTER 11

WHAT REWARDS WILL I RECEIVE?

Will There Be Material Rewards in Heaven?

"Reliable," he told us, "Volvos are one of the most reliable cars you can buy."

For the most part it was true . . . but not forever. Over two hundred thousand miles later the engine was still running (barely), but the rest of the car was junk. Road salt and Canada's freezing temperatures had done their worst. Rust was rampant.

"Look out! Keep your eyes on the road!"

"But I can't see where I'm going."

Not surprising, considering the hood had just blown open and was now obscuring my whole windshield. Suddenly there was a loud crack, followed by a massive "thunk" as the rusted-out hinges finally let go of the hood and it sailed into orbit behind us. Amazingly and fortunately there was nothing following us on the highway.

Needless to say, a week later I hauled the car to the junk yard. It didn't even have any trade-in value left. Yet only a few years earlier this beautiful, shiny new Volvo had been our pride and joy.

"But lay up for yourselves treasures in heaven, where neither moth nor rust doth corrupt" (Matt. 6:20).

111

What an amazing statement of Jesus. In heaven nothing we have will rust or wear out. No one will steal it either. Yes, you will enjoy material rewards of wealth, houses, lands and possessions (Psa. 112:3; Matt. 19:29; 24:47; 25:21). There is great treasure in heaven earned by generosity on earth toward others (Matt. 19:21; Luke 6:35,38; Heb.10:34).

Reserved for each of us in heaven is a special and glorious inheritance (1 Pet. 1:4). Proverbs tells us that house and riches are the inheritance of fathers (Prov. 19:14). God, our heavenly Father, has prepared a rich inheritance in glory for every child of His.

Though you may be wealthy beyond your wildest dreams it will seem almost insignificant beside the spiritual blessings of fellowship with God and your relationships to others. The material rewards are mere fringe benefits to living with Christ. Our possessions will no longer possess us. In heaven they will simply be things to take care of, to enjoy and praise God for, and to freely share with others.

Owning things is not evil of itself. It is our attitude towards possessions and our misuse of them that so often makes them sinful. The true joy of material wealth comes from acknowledging they are all a gift from God. We don't deserve them nor did we earn them without His help (and probably the help of countless others). This attitude frees us to truly enjoy them as precious entrustments rather than cling to them as self-earned idols. As someone once wisely said,

"You don't really own anything until you give it away."

You have to think about this one for a moment! It's a bit of a paradox. What it means is that if you are willing to freely part with something you posses, then you truly own it, it doesn't own you! So, yes, there will be material possessions and property ownership in heaven. Whether you are enjoying them yourself or freely sharing them with others, they will eternally remind you of the goodness of God. God gives us all *things* to enjoy. Did you know it is impossible to really enjoy riches and wealth for very long without God? (Eccl. 5:19).

112

Will There Be Degrees of Reward in Heaven?

Redistribution of wealth, evenly amongst everyone, is not a Biblical principle (Matt. 20:1-16). Remember heaven is a theocracy not a socialist utopia. There will be varying degrees of reward in heaven. The parable of the talents and the pounds clearly teaches this (Matt. 25:14-30; Luke 19:11-27). Some will have more than others.

No one will be unhappy with their lot in heaven, however. How come? Paul, speaking in the context of true wisdom vs worldly understanding, explains,

"Eye hath not seen, nor ear heard, neither have entered into the heart of man, the things God has prepared for them that love him" (1 Cor. 2:9).

God is not fair He is *just*. He always does (and gives) what is *right*. We will understand and be satisfied with His just rewards. All the riches and wealth of the universe belong to Christ and He shares it all with His bride, the church.

Like an inheritance today, we have not earned it nor do we specially deserve it. It is ours by birthright, the new birth of the spirit. Through Christ we have been adopted into God's family, and like any adoptee, we get to share in the family possessions.

There is one big difference, though. This inheritance can never be contested. It can never be taken away from you. It will never run out.

Yet heaven seems so far away and the mansions of earth (that others live in!) so desirous now. If only we could grasp the reality and richness of heaven. If only we would truly believe what the Bible promises, it would change our whole perspective.

There are some beautiful residential areas near where I live in Gulf Breeze, Florida. Magnificent golf-course and water-front homes line the quiet lanes and cul-de-sacs and shoreline. When I drive out-of-town visitors past these lovely mansions they will frequently ask,

"Doesn't it make you want to covet?"

"Not really. I'm looking forward to when I'll own a house far better than the best of these multi-million dollar homes. A home that will never be foreclosed on, broken into, destroyed by a hurricane, inherited by someone else, or fall into disrepair. I won't even have to pay taxes on it!"

The hope of heaven frees you to enjoy every good thing God has given (even to others), without having to covet and long for it yourself. I praise God for those He blesses with magnificent homes but the best is yet to come. Isn't this just a pious hope though? Does the Bible really say we will own property in heaven?

Will I Own Property in Heaven?

Isaiah saw God's people living on their own land in their own houses beside their own vineyards in eternity. Jesus told His disciples He was going to heaven to prepare homes for them. He also taught that those who left family, homes and material possessions for His sake would receive them back in abundance in eternity (Mark 10:29,30). The stewardship parables promise multiplied material as well spiritual rewards in heaven, for those who are faithful with what they are given on earth.

Property ownership was a principal reward for God's people entering the promised land. This reward and hope included the already established material possessions of the conquered Canaanites. The principles and responsibilities of property ownership were established in the Law, given to Moses. All of these things are a pattern, type and taste of heaven.

Nations are still a part of Christ's kingdom in heaven. The very fact that it is described as a kingdom implies designated territory, lands, for each country. Jesus' parable of the pounds promises that many will be given whole cities to be responsible for. Once again there is the clear indication of land ownership and control in heaven. Just remember that landlords will be righteous and humble (it must be heaven!). Maybe you will be one of them?

Adam was given a specific piece of land to take care of. His descendants were to populate and take care of the rest of the world, each therefore with his own land. Land ownership and responsibility is a fundamental principle of creation, the Law, the promised land, the millennial kingdom. . . and heaven.

Israel in particular will receive all the rewards of land and rule, given to them in the covenantal promises. The land promises will continue for them into eternity on the new earth. The very gates of the heavenly city, New Jerusalem, are marked with their tribal names and confirms that this city was built for them.

There are several major covenant promises made by God in the Bible that confirm specific rewards for eternity. Adam (Gen. 1:26-31), Noah (Gen. 9:9-17), Abraham (Gen. 17:1-8), Moses (Ex. 19:5-8), and David (2 Sam. 7:12-17; Psa. 89:3-4, 26-37), were all promised special, eternal blessings from God. Covenants are essentially unconditional. This simply means God makes them and God keeps them. Fulfillment doesn't depend on the response of the people.

However, the receipt and enjoyment of these promised rewards is conditional on the obedience and holiness of God's people. Many of the covenants carried parallel blessings and curses within them. The new and final covenant (1 Cor. 11:25; Heb. 9:15), confirmed by Christ's death and resurrection, completes and assures the fulfillment of all the previous covenants.

Only the shed blood of the Lamb of God, Jesus the Messiah, allows a holy God to consider anyone obedient or holy enough to even enter heaven, let alone receive all the promised rewards. A covenant, of course, is similar to a will. Someone has to die before a will takes effect and the inheritance is awarded. Jesus had to die before you could be assured of your inheritance in heaven (Heb. 9:15-17).

There are material as well as spiritual blessings assured in the covenants. Israel, for example, is promised ownership and control of all the land from the Euphrates river to the Nile (Deut. 11:24). These promises are eternal, not just for the millennium. This is yet another indication the New Earth will be similar to the old. Heaven is a tangible place with tangible assets to be enjoyed forever. Anyway, the greatest rewards in heaven are not material but relational. We will all enjoy these blessings forever and ever.

What Kind of Deeds on earth Are Rewarded in Heaven?

Character, obedience to God's word, submission to His will so He can conform you to the image of His Son, these gain great reward in heaven. The beatitudes are all about these things (Matt. 5:3-12). Faithfulness and trust earn special rewards also. Ministry for Christ, whether it be leading others to saving faith, being hospitable to a special servant of God, or simply giving a cup of water in kindness, all gain special rewards in heaven.

Anything and everything you let the spirit of Christ within you do on earth will be rewarded in heaven. Notice I am speaking of material and spiritual rewards to be received and enjoyed once you are in heaven. I am not talking about gaining entrance into heaven. That can never be earned. It is a free gift of God, received by faith and does not depend on anything special you have done.

Special crowns, symbols of position and power in heaven, are awarded to faithful believers. The New Testament lists several of these. An incorruptible crown is given to those who master self-control (1 Cor. 9:24-25). A crown of rejoicing comes to the soul winner (1 Thess. 2:19). For those who eagerly long for and look for Christ's return, they will be given a crown of righteousness (2 Tim. 4:8).

Overcoming difficulties, temptations and the trials of life through the power and love of Jesus secures a special reward of the crown of life (James 1;12). This same crown is also given to those willing to die for Christ (Rev. 2:10). Those who serve faithfully as Pastors and church leaders will be given a crown of glory (1 Pet. 5:1-4). The elders cast their crowns before Christ (Rev. 4:10), in recognition that it was only through His grace in their lives they were able to receive them. Nonetheless, each crown is eternal and represents the reward of a permanent position of power in heaven. The Bible tells us we will all receive the inheritance of eternal life, the blessings of God, the promises of God, and even share in the glory of God.

Faithfulness on earth, we have already seen, brings special status and reward in heaven. The repeated teaching of Jesus that many who are first (on earth) will be last in heaven, and vice versa, indicate that there is definite status conferred in heaven. The

116

wedding parables and their seating arrangements also bear this out. Daniel predicts that teachers (of God's word) and soul winners will have special status in heaven (Dan. 12:3). They will be the "stars" of eternity.

Remember that status, though it does bring privilege of responsibility and position in heaven, will not produce arrogance or snobbery. It is the humble, meek and lowly of earth that will be specially rewarded. God loves to honor those who honor Him. There will be many surprises in this area, I'm sure, when you see who is given status in heaven. They will be pleasant surprises, though, causing you great joy as you recognize the wisdom, mercy and grace of God.

Perhaps this concept rubs against our present understanding of fairness and equality. The Biblical teaching though is very clear. God does specially reward special effort and commitment. There are degrees of reward and status in heaven just as there are degrees of punishment in hell. That does not, in any way, make it less than heaven, or less than hell for anyone. Assuming you're headed for the former place, rest assured you will be very happy, and probably overwhelmingly surprised at your position and status in heaven.

"Seek first the kingdom of heaven and all these *things* will be added unto you."

If you make the spiritual a priority in your life then God promises to supply all your material needs, in this life and the next. "The kingdom of heaven is like . . ." Each of the parables Jesus begins with these words gives a clear picture not only of how precious and special heaven is but also reveals who will be there.

From the story of the sower, to the mustard seed, to the buried treasure and pearl of great price, to the laborers and the talents, and the illustration of the children, all of these give you a glimpse of heaven and the kind of people that will be there. True, Jesus uses symbols and types in the kingdom parables but a careful study of them gives you a taste of what heaven will be like. That indeed was the whole purpose of them, Jesus told His disciples (Matt. 13:10-11).

What Other Rewards Are There in Heaven?

Pleasure has become almost a dirty word amongst some Christians today, probably because pleasure is so often self-indulgent and sensual in our society. In heaven there is fullness of joy and (physical) pleasures forever more (Psa. 16:11). These pleasures must include the physical and material, for two of the greatest rewards in heaven will be a new and glorious physical body, and immortality.

Why would God give us physical bodies forever if there were not material rewards to enjoy forever with all of our physical senses? Yes, the greatest rewards and experiences of heaven will be the spiritual relationships. No, heaven is not just floating around in some spirit world, playing a harp! It is real. It is tangible. It is perfect. It is awesome!

Acceptance, unconditional and total, will be one of the emotional rewards of heaven. You'll never be snubbed. You'll never be ignored. You'll never be forgotten or overlooked in heaven. Fulfillment, total satisfaction with who you are and what you are doing, will be another emotional reward of living in heaven. Love, of course, perfect love from God Himself and from all those you will ever meet will surround you there.

You'll never worry again whether others like you or not. Everyone will be your best friend, including Jesus. They'll all love you up there. They'll all think you are very special, and treat you as such, because you already are in God's eyes. I told you that New Jerusalem was a city you'll never want to leave!

This is how God meant it to be for us from the beginning. This is how it can begin to be within the fellowship of true believers now. This is how it will be in heaven forever.

Peace, perfect inner peace will fill your soul in heaven. You will never be disturbed again in heart, mind, or spirit. Glory and power beyond imagination will be another of the spiritual rewards promised to all of Christ's followers. You'll never feel inadequate in heaven. Most of all you will get to personally fellowship with Jesus.

How everyone in heaven can each have personal contact with Jesus seems impossible from our present finite perspective. There would certainly be enough time in eternity for it. Just remember though, that your new body will be able to access the spiritual realms as well as the physical. Christ is bodily in the throne room of heaven right now but spiritually He is also omnipresent and in the hearts of all true believers everywhere.

Sure, we can't fully understand all of this but that's no reason not to believe what God has promised. After all who would have understood, or even believed you a hundred years ago if you tried to tell them one day half the world would simultaneously be able to watch a war being fought in the Persian Gulf, thanks to television, satellites and CNN? We just don't know enough yet. We particularly don't know God or understand the spiritual as we should and will one day.

Cities and land is what the Old Testament saints longed for in heaven. They looked forward to very tangible and earthlike rewards, though the book of Hebrews indicates that they knew these things would be heavenly, supernatural, and far better than they could ever imagine on earth. The Psalmist, prophets and patriarchs all believed God's promise of future prosperity for themselves and their nation, not just in the promised land or the millennial kingdom but in eternity.

The idea of prosperity in the Old Testament meant a general well being, of mind, body and spirit. It also included material blessings from God that could be enjoyed in a climate of peace and rest. Prosperity, in all of these aspects is very much a part of the rewards of heaven.

Rest, was one of the rewards the New Testament saints looked forward to also (Rev.13:14). They longed for fellowship with Christ again and with their brothers and sisters in the Lord and of course resurrection and new bodies (Phil. 3:20-21). Eternal life, with all of its connotations, was a paramount hope for the New Testament church.

The reward of living with Christ, of sharing His physical inheritance as well as His spiritual blessings encouraged the New Testament believers to faithful service and willingness to sacrifice even their lives. The apostle Paul in particular seemed to have such an excitement, desire and hope of heaven it enabled him to endure incredible hardships for his Lord and the cause of the gospel.

Oh! that we could catch some of Paul's enthusiasm for the reality of heaven's rewards, especially the reward of rest. Rest from our struggles, rest from our worries, rest from the consequences of our sin, rest from the selfish, hurtful attitudes and actions of others, these are some of the real rewards of heaven. It is this rest, symbolized in the Sabbath, that makes all the other blessings of heaven, spiritual and physical, so special and enjoyable.

Let's look then at this Sabbath rest principle that is so much a part of the Biblical view of heaven.

CHAPTER 12

THE SABBATH REST PRINCIPLE

What Does the Sabbath Point To?

"Weekends are free. We won't be working cargo. You can go stay with your friends in Christchurch if you want to. I don't need you here."

The First Mate noticed my puzzled look.

"This is New Zealand, Larry. Nobody works on Sunday and just about everything except the corner store is shut down."

"How come?" I asked.

"They still have Sabbath Laws (it was the early 60's). I think it's because of the strong, Plymouth Brethren religious influence. Actually it is kind of nice because I've noticed it encourages a lot more family time together than we see back home. Of course the younger generation think it's *too* quiet and restful on weekends."

What a contrast to the twenty-four hour, seven days a week shopping, the Sunday sports, the scattered families, and the perpetual, money-grabbing commerce of today? Whatever happened to Sunday family lunch after church? Yet survey after survey in the past has shown a six-day working week is much more efficient and productive than seven days. Apparently God knew what He was doing when He instituted the Sabbath Day rest!

Yet man in his wisdom thinks he can do better than God. In fact he thinks he doesn't really need God at all, so why take a day off to worship and thank Him? Why relax when you can have it all now? The one with the most toys wins, so go for the gusto, grab what you can while you can. You're the master of your own destiny. You only go round once. And mankind misses what Sunday after Sunday is pointing to.

Heaven is described, even defined as a place of rest. Did you realize every Sunday of every week is supposed to remind you of the hope of heaven? The enjoyment of rest, worship and family time each Sunday is meant to give you a weekly taste of heaven. God rested on the seventh day of creation. No, He didn't cease all activity. He still sustained what He had created but now He took time to enjoy His creative work, and see it was good. He took time to fellowship with His special creation, man.

God had completed His work. It was finished. So He rested and blessed the seventh day, making it Holy and special forever (Gen. 2:1-3). We are to keep it holy and special also, for our own benefit as much as for pleasing God. When we make it different from the work-a-day world, when we take time to rest and thank God for His blessings we are reminded life will be different one day. There is hope. There is a heaven.

What is the "Rest" of Heaven?

Work was still a part of Adam's life even before the fall. So what was the "rest" of Eden? Before God cursed the ground after Adam sinned, even Adam's work was restful and fulfilling. He also enjoyed the *rest* of God's presence, of walking and talking with Him every day. Resting in the security of knowing God had already provided all his needs was a part of Eden too. Until he disobeyed God, Adam also rested in the hope of living forever.

Eden, then, is a type or picture of the *rest* of heaven; enjoyable work, material abundance, the presence of God, and immortality. When you take Sunday to enjoy the fruit of your labors, and enter His house of worship to thank Him for His abundant provision, it continually renews your hope of heaven, as well as your dependence upon Him.

Work, since the fall, is a necessary struggle we have to engage in just to survive. When Sunday becomes the same as every other day of the week as far as industry and commerce is concerned, we deny ourselves the hope of the daily grind ever ending. It becomes increasingly hard then for a society to even believe there is a heaven and a better world to come.

"There remaineth therefore a rest to the people of God" (Heb 4:9).

This passage of Hebrews (Heb. 4:1-11) clearly equates the Sabbath rest with heaven. It parallels it with the rest of the promised land too. So what was the rest of the promised land for Israel?

Prepared, already built cities and houses was part of the *rest* from nomadic, desert tent living for Israel when they entered Canaan. The abundance of fruit, cattle, wheat fields and vineyards was part of the hoped for *rest* in the promised land. A sense of national identity as God's people in their own permanent land was also part and parcel of the *rest* promised to them.

Each of these things, as Sabbath rest types, point to heaven. If Israel had continued to obey God, once in the land, then He would have given them permanent rest from their enemies too. A pre-built city, material needs in abundance, identity with God forever, are all part and parcel of heaven, the final rest for God's people.

Yet a whole generation of God's people never even entered the promised land the first time, except for Joshua and Caleb.

"Let us labor therefore to enter into that rest, lest any man fall after the same example of unbelief" (Heb. 4:11).

Fulfillment of all the land and throne promises given to the patriarchs was the rest Israel was looking for in the Millennial kingdom. This peace and prosperity would be ushered in by the Messiah. With Jerusalem and the whole world under His control Israel would finally receive the rest they had hoped for since first entering the promised land.

123

This is why even the disciples of Jesus were hoping He would throw off the Roman yoke and set up His earthly kingdom. This is why they were so confused and disappointed when He went to the cross. Yet it is in the cross and the resurrection that God completes His covenant promises. Because of His Son's sacrifice for the sin of mankind, God can now accept (indeed declares) everyone, who puts their faith in Christ, as perfect, holy and obedient enough to enter heaven's rest.

The Millennium is a unique picture of Sabbath rest. Under Christ's one thousand year perfect rule the earth's ecology is restored. The natural world is redeemed and at rest for the first time since the fall. Even the animals are at rest from each other. Nations turn their weapons into ploughshares in the Millennium so there is political rest too. Perfect government, perfect environment, perfect peace and abundance. What a foretaste of heaven!

What Was the Purpose of the Sabbath for Israel?

Holiness was the essence of the Sabbath for Old Testament Israel. It was part of the Ten Commandments (Ex.20:8-11). Even the servants, animals and strangers among them were to enjoy physical rest on the Sabbath. It was also a day of worship included as one of the feasts of the Lord, along with the Passover, feast of tabernacles and day of atonement (Lev. 23: 1-44).

Holy literally means "separate from" or other than" and the keeping of the Sabbath separated Israel from the surrounding nations. It made them stand out and stand apart as God's special people. In fact this holy separation was so important for Israel to learn that God instructs Moses to institute the death penalty for any who deliberately violated this Sabbath commandment (Ex. 31:14-15).

In contrast to this harsh punishment there is a special blessing of prosperity promised to all those who faithfully honor the Sabbath (Isa. 58:13-14). This principle still holds true for all God's people. Read what Isaiah says. This is why Nehemiah's reforms focused heavily on a restoration of the Sabbath laws so God would start to bless the returning remnant (Neh. 13: 15-22).

Teaching the word of God on the Sabbath, was Jesus' practice. He faithfully attended the synagogue to do this (Mark 1:2). Luke tells us it was His custom to teach in the synagogue on the Sabbath in His home town of Nazareth (Luke 4:16). He did the same in Capernaum (Luke 4:31), and whenever He ministered in other Jewish towns.

Jesus was following the custom of His godly parents in faithfully keeping all the feasts of Israel, including the Sabbath (cf Luke 2:42). He was also obeying the commandments. Notice Jesus faithfully attends the local church even though most of them were corrupted by years of Rabbinic, unscriptural traditions. Once again, the principle of keeping the Sabbath rest is more important than the religious rituals. Jesus tried to show the synagogue leaders that their rituals were missing the whole point of the Sabbath. But they wouldn't listen.

Healing, casting out demons, gathering food on the Sabbath got Jesus into trouble with the religious leaders. They accused Him of breaking Sabbath law. Jesus skillfully turned their arguments against them by quoting the written word of God, to show their twisted additions to Mosaic law were both hypocritical and false (Matt. 12:2-8;10-12).

Remembering the Sabbath is supposed to point us to the rest of heaven we can begin to understand why Jesus was so upset with the religious rulers and their rules. They had made the Sabbath something to be endured rather than looked forward to. The Sabbath was meant for man (for his benefit), not man for the Sabbath (Mark 2:27). Jesus also declared He was Lord of the Sabbath (Mark 2:28).

This statement angered the religious leaders even more because they knew it meant He was God. Think about it. Sabbath means rest. Jesus is the one who says,

"Come unto me and I will give you rest" (Matt. 11:28).

Only through Him can we experience the rest of heaven. Keeping the Sabbath then, not only reminds us of heaven but points us to the King of heaven, Jesus.

What's the Difference Between Sabbath and Sunday?

Saturday, of course, is the equivalent of the Jewish Sabbath as it is the last day of the week. So why do Christians worship on Sunday which happens to be the first day of the week? Jesus rose from the dead on the first day of the week and this became known in the early New Testament church as the Lord's Day (Rev. 1:10)

The Sabbath was part of the Old Covenant (Mosaic Law). The Lord's Day, Sunday, is part of the New Covenant (1 Cor. 11:25) and therefore replaced Saturday observance for the early church. The principle of the Sabbath rest, however, is eternal for it goes back to creation. God is more concerned with us keeping the principle than with the specific day of the week

It is significant to note in Genesis when God *finished* and *completed* His work of creation He rested on the last day of the week, Saturday (Gen. 2:1-2). On the cross Jesus declared His work of redemption was *finished* (John 19:30). On the Lord's day, Sunday, when Jesus rose from the dead, God *completed* the New Covenant by accepting Christ's sacrifice for man's sin, once and for all. So now, as it were, God *rested* from His redemptive work on the first day of the week, Sunday.

Theologically, of course, God had already completed His work of salvation even before creation, in the Lamb slain from the foundation of the world (Rev. 13:8). So in a sense the last day for creation (Saturday) and the first day for Redemption (Sunday) become one in Jesus Christ, the Alpha and Omega. You can begin to see now just how important the Sabbath rest principle is to God, and to our understanding of heaven.

Worship for the New Testament church, therefore, was now celebrated on the first day of the week (Acts 20:7; 1 Cor. 16:1-2). One of its purposes was to separate these new believers from traditional Judaism. It was also a reminder of the resurrection, that they now worshipped and served a risen Lord, not just a dead patriarch.

It is interesting to note the only use of the term "Lord's Day" is by John in the Book of Revelation. It is on this day, Sunday, John sees and writes about heaven! Remember the *rest* principle of the Sabbath (now Sunday) is to confirm your hope of heaven.

I know many of you, in essential services, have to work on Sunday, and this is ok. Jesus taught it is better to do good than evil on the Sabbath. It's not the day so much as the principle which is important. That is to set some time aside, when you're not working or on another day of the week, to rest, relax, and worship God in His house.

I know we can worship the Lord anywhere but church is where it's at, the Bible teaches (Heb. 10:25). Worshipping on the Lord's Day outside of the body of Christ will not renew your hope or vision of heaven. It will not be a true Sabbath (heavenly) experience for you.

Spiritual refreshment on a regular basis is vital to our well being. Without this we struggle, physically and emotionally to get through the tough times. This is why the Sabbath rest principle is so important. I am sure you have read newspaper and magazine studies showing that people who regularly attend church live longer and have happier marriages.

Why is this? Because God made the Sabbath for man's benefit. But only those who observe Sunday rest and worship reap the rewards. They are better able to rest from the worries of the week. Sunday worship renews their faith, their perspective, their priorities and their hope. Heaven becomes much more real and attainable when you keep the fourth commandment.

God's *rest* is the promise of heaven, the Book of Hebrews teaches. The Sabbath therefore, is a type of heaven (Heb. 4:3-5). Faith is the key to entering God's rest (Heb. 4:2,3,6,9,11). The promised land is a type of Sabbath rest but is not the final heaven (Heb. 4:6-9). And like Israel entering the promised land, where a whole generation never made it because of disobedience and idolatry, so not everyone automatically gets to go to heaven.

This fascinating chapter of Hebrews equates the Sabbath and its rest with the eternal rest of heaven. This rest (eternal life) begins at the moment of faith in God's Son. At salvation we cease from our own works as Christ begins to work in us and through us (Heb. 4:10). This special day of the week then is more than just a day of physical rest. It is day of hope, and salvation, renewal, and commitment.

127

What Other Types of Sabbath Rest Are There?

Complete entrance into the *rest* of heaven comes the day you receive your new, glorified body. Then you will enjoy the physical rest and freedom of heaven. No more sickness, sorrow or pain. No more headaches, heartaches, or weariness. Just the incredible joy of being alive, forever and ever.

Everything which stresses you out now, will be removed. Imagine being free from the pressures of hunger, thirst, fear, hopelessness, frustration, lack of time, lack of money, lack of resources, lack of understanding friends, lack of appreciation, lack of sleep? I'm sure you could add a few more to the list. It will be the most restful forever you could ever dream of. Better than the best Sunday you've ever spent!

I don't know about you, but I'm looking forward to this kind of rest. "Even so, come quickly, Lord Jesus." The physical rewards won't be shabby either. Believe me (or better yet, the Bible!), you will have the best of everything. Jesus promises it. Sunday confirms it.

All the types of heaven we have mentioned give us clues as to the specifics of heaven's rest. Eden reminds us there will be no more "sweat of the brow" labor in heaven. The ground will be no longer cursed. The promised land reminds us that we will have freedom from our enemies. There will be eternal rest from even the threat of war in heaven. There will be no violence or fighting there.

The millennium reminds us that we will rest from any fear of wild animals. They will all be vegetarian and tame in heaven. Even the Tabernacle reminds us that, under the New Covenant, we are already free from impossible-to-keep religious rituals, and will be in heaven too. The principles, of holiness, faith and obedience, that were behind the rituals, will of course remain.

Communion and fellowship with God, face to face and forever, will be part of the spiritual rest of heaven. No more will selfishness, pride, laziness or un-confessed sin get in the way. The struggle to put to death your old nature, striving to live in total surrender to Christ will be over. You will be spiritually free and at rest with Him, forever.

Even the battle to witness to the lost will be over. You can rest assured that everyone going to be there is there. This is one thing we won't have to work at in heaven, and that is soul winning. You'll never have to worry again about the spiritual condition of your loved ones or your neighbors. Just think, you'll never have to worry again about anything. Everything and everyone will be perfect! So will we need Sundays in heaven?

Worship is one of the primary activities in heaven. In the throne room of God it is continuous, and a daily occurrence for the saints. Sunday is a type of heaven, so in a sense heaven will be a continuous week of Sundays. Every day in heaven will seem like a Sunday is supposed to be now, restful, worshipful and family orientated.

Because of the consistent mention of days, months and years in relation to eternity we will still have weeks. Therefore there will still be Sundays marking the progression of time. The Bible refers to the Sabbath as a feast. The feasts are to be remembered forever. Sunday therefore will still be a special day of rest and worship, different from the rest of the week.

Realize we are drawing on Biblical principles and patterns here not just individual verses. With regards to the days of the week and measuring time in heaven we will look at this in greater depth. Is there time in heaven? Or is time no more? Is everything in a constant *present* or is time simply irrelevant? Will the past be remembered? Will anything age in heaven? Is time-travel possible?

CHAPTER 13

ALL ABOUT TIME AND ETERNITY

How Do You Define Eternity?
.Endless days and endless nights of doing whatever we chose. Walking, swimming, sunbathing, exploring, dining, shopping, whenever we felt like it. Two whole weeks of freedom. The days melted into one another. Time stood still. Suddenly it was over!

"Don't you wish this could last forever?"

"I do. But it can't. We'd better pack up and leave now or we'll miss the plane," replied my ever practical wife.

"But just think, if this were heaven it could go on forever and ever!"

"I know but wouldn't we get bored after a while? I'm not sure I'm looking forward to things going on forever and ever. The endlessness of heaven is a little frightening to me."

She's right. We are so bound by time on this earth and so used to there always being an end to everything. If we are honest, the thought of eternity scares most of us. Will life really just go on and on and on?

How is eternity defined? Is it just endlessness? In which case how can you possibly find enough to do forever and ever? Or is time simply irrelevant given the spiritual nature of our new bodies.

Or is there progression and measurement of time, with events starting and ending and new ones beginning again?

Knowing God and His Son Jesus Christ is the Bible's definition of eternal life. This of itself implies a progression of knowledge and discovery and therefore of time. Will it really take forever to find out God? Of course, else He wouldn't be God anymore. You would be!

We have seen how man will take care of nature on the new earth, just as Adam did in the beginning. This will be part and parcel of discovering the glory of God, of knowing Him. Do you know now, how many species of birds there are, or butterflies, or even mammals?

If you observed, cared for and learned everything there is to know about just one animal it could take several lifetimes. If you studied every single species it could easily take up millions of years, just on this one project. To read the books or watch the videos of someone else who did could also take up a very long time. In eternity you'll have the time.

Or think about this one. If you've lived with someone for fifty years there would still be things you didn't know or understand about them, wouldn't there? Imagine trying to get to know a million people as well as you think you know your spouse? Or try a billion people? You'll need fifty billion years and you still won't know them completely. Finally, however, you'll have the opportunity to develop those friendships you just didn't have time for here. You'll need forever! You will have forever.

Then there's the task of getting to know Christ Himself, in all of His fullness. No, you won't get bored in heaven. You will always need more time. You will always have the time.

Is Time Important in Heaven?

Knowledge requires the passage of time to acquire it. Hope also, along with faith and love, remains forever (1 Cor. 13:13), and demands the progression of time. It requires a definite future. Remember the music filling heaven's throne room? You can't make music without timing. So time is very important in heaven in terms of progression, completion, and fulfillment. On the other hand, being in eternity, you won't be bound by time. You will no longer be a slave to the second hand. Time after all, is relative, especially in heaven. To God a thousand years are but one day and one day a thousand years (2 Pet. 3:8).

Time seemed to stand still on our vacation when we had no time restraints. So in heaven there will be times (excuse the pun) when time will be irrelevant. It will seem to stand still, be ever present, just as it is to God. Even now, in your finite state, time can appear to go into slow motion. When sudden trauma, such as a car crash, occurs it can trigger powerful hormones to the brain that literally give you time to take life saving actions within a split second.

So if time is relative and life in heaven is a kind of eternal present will you be aware of the passage of time? How will it be measured?

Day, in the Scriptures refers mostly to a literal solar day. Depending on the context it can also point to a period of time such as the *day* of Jacob's trouble. In heaven time is measured in days (Psa. 89:29; Rev. 7:15), and even hours (Rev. 8:1). The fruit on the tree of life in heaven is produced every *month*. The sun and the moon continue in heaven (Psa. 89:36,37) confirming the fact of days and months.

There are books and records of the past, including the Bible, in heaven. So the previous passage of time is still measured and remembered in heaven. The continuing passage of time will still be measured in similar fashion, in days, months, and years. The difference will be your perception of time. Being spiritual, being perfect, and content with your days, and under no time restraints of any kind, everything will seem to be in the present.

The passing of time won't upset you anymore. After all, what's a thousand years in eternity? Like it is for God, it will seem to you as yesterday. Yet it will have passed. Achievements will have been made and projects accomplished and new ones begun. You will go on from glory to glory.

Remember we talked about everything you do now still happening somewhere out there in time and space? The terms *past, present, future*, really do become relative. It all depends on where you are in the universe. It may even depend on how fast you are traveling at the time! Are you going faster or slower than light?

Blows your mind doesn't it? Some of you have probably taken a *time-out* at this point! My purpose was not to confuse you but simply to remind you in eternity we will view time from a vastly different perspective than we do now, even though it will still be measured. But doesn't the Bible say time will be no more?

John does indeed write "there should be time no longer" (Rev. 10:6). He uses the same Greek word *eti* with a negative as in *no more* sea. In the context of this passage John is simply referring to God's work of judgment being finished (cf Rev. 16:17; 21:6). He is saying there is no more time *left* before the mystery of God (v7) is completed. Time itself continues.

John writes about there being no night and no sun (Rev. 22:5) in the heavenly city. This could imply that because there are no solar days in New Jerusalem the passage of time is not measured any more. However, he also sees the martyred tribulation saints worshipping God in the throne room of heaven, *day and night* (Rev. 7:15). Time (at least relative to the new earth), for the martyrs in heaven continues. It is still measured by days and months and years.

Nowhere else in Scripture does it refer to time ceasing. In many, many places the Bible refers to day and months and years in reference to eternal things. After all, God created time as part of the universe. Like the universe, it too will continue into eternity. There will be time in heaven. Interestingly God created time to be measured in days and nights, even before he hung the sun and moon in space (Gen. 1:3-5)?

Will There Be Day and Night in Heaven?

Darkness and clouds surround the throne of God (Psa. 97:2). Yet John tells us there will be no night there (Rev. 21:25). The very source of light emanates from the throne, from Christ who is the light. The sun and moon continue forever yet there is no sunlight in the throne room (Rev. 21:23). What does all this mean? Some of this we have explained back in chapter 5. So will there be days and nights in heaven?

First of all the darkness and the light are alike to God (Psa. 139:12). He can penetrate the darkness as though it were light. Second, from a physical perspective, light is only seen as light in contrast to the darkness. In your glorified, spirit controlled body you will be able to see in the darkness. You will be able to bring the light of Christ even to the blackness of outer space if you choose.

Yes, there will be darkness in contrast to the light. Yes, it will always seem like day in the heavenly city because of the glory of God there. Remember the pillar of fire in the wilderness, a symbol of the light of Christ? Or the glow on Moses' face after he'd been in the presence of the glory of God? In your new body you will be able to enjoy the display of light in the heavenly city yet still see the dark clouds and the blackness of space.

The stars continue into eternity. How can you enjoy their brilliance if there is no night? Given the continued measurement of time in days and months and years there will still be days and nights in heaven, at least on the new earth. Remember also, day and night were created by God before the sun, moon and stars! The sun, moon and stars were to separate the day and night and to be for signs and seasons (Gen 1:14).

God promised Noah day and night would continue as long as the earth (Gen 8:22). Some would say this means only as long as *this* earth remains. Jeremiah's prophesies, however, indicate this covenant promise of day and night to be an eternal one (Jer. 33:20-21, 25). Also, the covenant with Noah was confirmed with the *eternal* covenant of the rainbow (Gen.9:16). Significantly, there is a rainbow around the eternal throne of God in heaven!

The Jeremiah passage points to the millennial kingdom and the eternal rule of Messiah through David's line. God tells Jeremiah the covenant of the day and night can no more be broken than the eternal covenant with David (cf Psa. 89:29, 36, 37). The covenant of the day refers to creation (Gen.1:3-5, 14-18), and to the restatement of this covenant given to Noah (Gen. 8:22). Like the Davidic covenant it is irrevocable. If this is so then here's another indication that God has planned all along to make the New Earth in heaven very similar to this one.

"While the earth remaineth, seedtime and harvest, and cold and heat, and summer and winter, and day and night shall not cease" (Gen. 8:22).

During the flood, many of these things did cease, temporarily. This is why God has to reassure Noah of His creation covenant. They resumed again as Noah resettled the earth. During the traumatic upheavals of the tribulation judgments, many of them will cease again. They will resume during the millennial kingdom.

At the end of the millennial kingdom when the earth is burned up, these promised cycles will cease again, momentarily. In heaven, on the new, restored earth, these eternal covenant promises of God will resume forever just as they have before. Though *this* earth will not remain unchanged (Psa. 102:25-27), the earth does remain forever (Psa.78:69).

Seasons are part of the eternal covenant given to Noah. The Sun and moon regulate the seasons on earth, and were created for such a purpose. They will again on the new earth, so it can bring forth its abundance for the blessings of God's people.

God's promise to Noah included the continuance of seedtime and harvest, cold and heat, summer and winter. The seasons on the new earth will no longer be affected by man's sin, as in the past. They will be far better than the best of weather patterns you have yet seen.

What an incredible world we have to look forward to in heaven. We will still be able to enjoy the beauty of the snow, the grandeur of the ice, the warmth of the sun, and the fragrance of the rain. The contrast of the seasons will still cause us to thank God and stand in awe of Him. Time will still be measured in months and years, in planting and harvesting, day after day and night after night throughout eternity. But will times past be remembered?

Will the Past Be Remembered?

Scars in the hands and side of Jesus' resurrected body convinced Thomas it was really Him. Records and books of the past are kept in heaven. The Bible itself is preserved forever (Psa. 119:89; Isa. 30:8). Things of the past are remembered in heaven.

The Bible contains the history of God's dealings with His people. It will be read and remembered in heaven. The scars of Jesus will cause you to remember His sacrifice and death. The significant events that brought glory to God will be remembered in heaven. Your sins of the past will not be remembered. Not that God can ever lose His memory. But He promises to choose to forget them. He wills them out of existence.

Will we remember the past? Anything that was Christ honoring will be remembered. Everything else will either be removed from our memories or we will, like God, choose to forget them. Isaiah suggests that we will be so enamored with the new heavens and earth, we won't stop to consider the past. Everything in heaven will be so much better than anything we could have remembered (Isa. 65:17-18).

Obviously the records and books in the libraries of heaven will tell us of the past. History, however, will be viewed and recorded from a whole new perspective. Everything about the past will be seen in terms of the central figure of history, Jesus Christ. You will finally see man's history as it really is. The future history of eternity will be remembered in terms of knowing more and more about God.

Perfection is one of the promises, qualities and qualifications for heaven. So nothing will visibly age, wear out or deteriorate (become imperfect) there. Everything, however, will be in existence for longer and longer, as far as the passage of recorded time. There will be change and progression, therefore, in heaven.

God originally created the mountains, for example, with the appearance of age. He spoke and they came into being, instantly, like everything else in creation. So in heaven many things may have the appearance of age but there will be no subsequent deterioration. If there were, then these things would not be perfect. They would not be complete. They would not be in heaven.

What a contrast to our world today. A huge amount of time and an even larger amount of money is spent on maintenance and repairs. Things wear out and eventually have to be replaced. Billions of dollars are spent every year trying to recapture our youth and prevent the inevitable signs of aging. All to no avail.

Heaven won't be like that. Everything will look as new and be kept in perfect working order. Most of all, your own body will remain forever young and in perfect working order. Hallelujah! An impossible dream? While sin and death still reign, yes. But Christ has conquered death and paid for sin. He came back from the dead to prove heaven is real. He offers eternal life to everyone. Best of all it's free!

What Things from this Life Will Be in Heaven?

"Naked came I out of my mother's womb, and naked shall I return thither," Job writes (Job 1:21). You take nothing with you into heaven. You will need nothing from this life in heaven. Why? Because Christ makes all things new for you (Rev. 21:5).

Job had a lot of stuff. He was the Bill Gates of his day because God had blessed him. Yet he recognized they were just temporary loans from God. We all die eventually. All the things we have accumulated will pass on to others or be destroyed. We can't take them with us. The whole universe one day will be burned up and renewed. There won't be a thing left from this old world.

So why do we spend so much time and money on temporary things? Well, you have to live, and what's wrong with trying to make this life more enjoyable? Nothing, if this life is all there is. But it isn't. Heaven exists. Heaven is real and it lasts a long, long time. So does hell.

In heaven there will be no more tears, no more dying, nor sorrow or crying, nor any pain. These things will be done away with (Rev. 21:4). Not so in hell. Well, is there anything you can take with you into heaven?

Relationships are the only things you can take with you into heaven. First your relationship with Christ. This, after all, is the only way into heaven. Second, your reputation and character, your faithfulness, if you like, to Christ. Third, your relationships to others in the Lord.

The latter would include those you have been privileged enough to lead to salvation, your spiritual children. It would also include all those you have given a cup of cold water to in Christ's name, starting them on the road to salvation. Believing spouses and close

138

friends in the Lord would be part of these relationships also. And, of course, every fellow-believer you have ever served with or discipled will have an ongoing relationship with you in heaven.

We will discuss this relationship principle further in a later chapter. For now let's consider what this means. Christ, and the lives you have touched in His name, will be the only things (persons) you will see in heaven from this old earth. True character, of course, comes only from a relationship with Jesus Christ. What does this say about the time we should be spending developing these relationships now?

Is Time Travel Possible in Heaven?

Speaking of spending time in heaven, the question inevitably arises about the possibility of time travel. Will we be able to travel into the past or future? This question, of course, deals with an area of speculation rather than clear Biblical teaching. However, it's worth considering in the light of what we have already gleaned from Scripture about time.

Time is measured and time progresses in heaven. Yet past, present and future are all eternal present to God. He is the great *I Am* God. Eternally present and intimately concerned and personally involved with His people. He knows the end from the beginning. History is still happening to God. The future has already been accomplished in His eyes.

Yes, you are made in God's image but you will never be exactly as He is. You will not become omnipresent in heaven, nor omniscient (knowing everything), nor omnipotent (all powerful and in control of everything). We will not have control over time. We will not be able to change the past or the future. You may however, as God allows, be able to transcend time for His purposes. What do I mean by that?

Well, you will have a new, spiritual body able to transport itself instantly to anywhere in the universe. This is what Christ demonstrated in His resurrected body and you will be like Him in this respect. As far as we understand today, if it were possible to travel faster than light, theoretically you would go back in time. In the spiritual realm you may be able to accomplish this!

If the past really does keep on going in time and space then (in theory), you would be able to instantly travel to where the light from the particular past you have chosen will have just arrived. Then you could indeed observe the past as it is happening, but not be able to interact with it. Only God can do that.

Let me boggle your mind even more! With the advent of space travel we have apparently proved the human body ages slower, the faster it travels. So astronauts return to earth measurably younger than their counterparts on earth. Time, as it were slows down for them. In a sense they have come back to a future earth?

Well in heaven there is no aging anyway and you can travel as fast as light (or maybe even faster). Time becomes relative. Time can be transcended. If it brings glory to God and increases our knowledge of Him, you will indeed be able to engage in some form of time travel. What amazing things are in store for you in heaven, things beyond imagining! Does this mean, then, you can know the future in heaven?

Perfection in heaven does not include omniscience (knowing everything). So you cannot know the future as God knows it. Even Jesus, while on earth, did not know the exact hour of His future return (Matt. 24:36). As your understanding of God increases, however, so will your ability to predict what will happen based on a complete trust in what God has said.

Given the spiritual dimension of heaven and our new perspective on time, the question is somewhat redundant. If we really will be able to move through time, then the future becomes less important to us except as it causes us to praise and glorify God. But from a finite perspective, think about this.

If everyone is totally obedient to Christ and perfect in all that they do, then anything once begun will always be completed (unlike today!). It will happen in the future in the exact way and exact time Jesus has instructed it to be. In this way you will certainly be able to accurately predict the future in heaven.

Well, won't this take away the fun of eternity? Not at all. You still won't know what the completed project will lead to or what wonders Christ has in store for you after this? Remember, the Bible promises the pleasures continue for evermore.

What Does the Bible Say Lasts Forever?

Israel lasts forever, the land and the people. The earth, we have seen, lasts forever, changed but similar. Christ's promised kingdom continues forever in eternity. The Old Testament lists many things that are timeless and will reappear in heaven.

It makes a fascinating study to see what the Bible specifically says lasts forever and therefore will be in heaven. They give us a much clearer picture of what heaven will be like. Most of them we have already touched on in the previous chapters. God's word, the Sabbath, Jerusalem, the sun, moon and stars, mountains and hills, rainbows, the sanctuary of God, Christ's government, inheritance and blessings, to name but a few.

Then there are the intangibles, forever part of heaven. Things like peace, love, forgiveness, salvation, glory, joy, mercy, satisfaction, faithfulness, righteousness, truth. These are but a few of the blessings that last forever and will therefore be part of heaven.

Faith, hope and love, the New Testament assures us last forever. Yes, there will be hope in heaven and much to look forward to. The saints, of course last forever. You will never be kicked out of heaven. Christ's kingdom lasts forever and we will help Him rule forever in heaven.

Jesus promises that our homes will last forever in heaven (Luke 16:9). God's presence and His throne will be with us forever. It is this promise in particular, of an everlasting relationship to God that makes heaven so special. Never again will you feel cut off from God. Never again will your relationship to Him be marred or diminished in anyway. It will grow and last forever, the fulfillment of what you were created for in the first place.

We have talked much about the physical and material joys of heaven, and discussed time and eternity and the intangible, mind stretching wonders to come. The greatest wonder of all will be your relationships in heaven. Will I really see God? Will we really see our loved ones? What about the angels?

PART IV.

A NEW RELATIONSHIP

CHAPTER 14

WILL I SEE GOD ?

Is God Visible in the Throne Room of Heaven?

Queen Elizabeth II had recently been crowned. Once a year she visited my home town of Epsom, just south of London. She came there to watch her thoroughbred horses race in the Derby. On this occasion the motorcade stopped briefly outside our tiny parochial school. We were all lined up in front of the school yard in our best uniforms to greet her. As the new Head of State, the Queen was automatically head of the Church of England as well.

It's all kind of a blur now, but I remember the incredible excitement we felt at being face to face with royalty. How tiny she looked! Somehow the newspaper articles and photos (few people had television then), had made us expect someone larger than life. She smiled at everyone shook hands with some and even talked briefly with two of the children in our line up. Then she was gone.

Afterwards, we were each presented with a silver teaspoon complete with Royal Crest. It was to commemorate her visit and her coronation. This little spoon was the only thing we kids had to remind us we had actually met the sovereign of our country face to face. What a moment! What a privilege! What an experience for a young child!

One day you will meet the sovereign of the universe. He will seem larger than life. In fact He will appear so bright and so Holy, so powerful and awesome you will instinctively fall down before Him (Rev. 1:17). For this is not the temporary sovereign of a small island nation. This is the eternal King of Kings and Lord of Lords. What a moment! What a privilege! What an experience to look forward to!

God will be very visible in heaven. You will see Him face to face in the person of Jesus Christ, seated on the throne. Christ is the image of the invisible God (Col.1:15; Heb.1:3). In Him dwells all the fullness of the Godhead, bodily (Col. 2:9). God the Father is spirit and so too is the Holy Spirit, obviously. They are physically invisible. The third person of the Godhead, the Son, has a visible, physical body. The complete Trinity dwells in Him.

"But I want to see God in heaven, not just Jesus," people often protest.

Philip wanted to see God also. He demanded Jesus show him the Father. Jesus berated him for his lack of understanding. He told him anyone who saw Him (Jesus), had already seen the Father (John 14: 7-11). This is because the Father and the Holy Spirit dwell in Jesus. And Jesus is God.

It's a little bit like someone asking to see your personality, or your mind. "I want to see the real you," they protest. Well, that's pretty hard to do without showing them your physical person first. They have to meet you physically, listen to your voice, and watch you in action, in order to see the real you. Over time, they will get to *see* your personality, mind, and even spirit. They are there all the time, in your physical person. They haven't jumped to someone else!

"Let us make man in *our* image," God said (Gen. 1:26).

The *our* refers to the Trinity. Similar to God we have three aspects to our one person; body, soul (mind, will, emotions), and spirit. Unlike us, God is not three parts in one person. Somehow He is three complete and separate persons in one body and person of the Son. Not that anyone can ever adequately explain the Trinity, but it's there in Scripture, so we know it is true. Yes, you will see God, the Bible assures us.

146

"In my flesh shall I see God. Whom I shall see for myself, and mine eyes shall behold" (Job 19:26-27).

You will know it is the Father and the Spirit, as well as the Son. The whole Godhead will be there on that magnificent throne in New Jerusalem. He will dwell with us forever.

Will God Live Physically with Man in Heaven?

Mansions abound, Jesus said, in His father's house. The whole idea here is of the bridegroom preparing a house to live in with his wife on his father's estate. Continuing this Jewish wedding theme there is the great marriage feast planned for us in heaven, that we've talked about already. After all of the initial celebrations, and all the presents (rewards) are opened you then live happily ever after with Christ, helping Him rule His kingdom.

God lives physically with us in heaven. This is what the prophets looked forward to much more than for the land and material blessings of heaven. Jehovah God would one day come to earth and live permanently among His people. Once again there are a progression of types and fulfillments of this hope and promise in Scripture.

Before the fall, Adam and Eve enjoyed the physical presence of God walking with them in the garden. Israel enjoyed the physical evidence of God's presence among them in the pillar of fire and cloud leading them for forty years in the wilderness. The New Testament refers to this being the very spirit of Christ (1 Cor. 10:2-4).

Then the Messiah came. For a little while God lived physically amongst His people. But they rejected Him and sent Him to the cross. He (Jesus) willingly gave up His life so mankind might still have the opportunity to live forever with God. Being God and being totally obedient as the Son of man, death could not hold Him and He rose again bodily from the grave to return to heaven.

One day the Scriptures promise Christ will return to earth, first for His church, and then to set up His kingdom on earth. For one thousand years God will once again live physically among His people. At the conclusion of this millennium whole nations of men will again reject Him. The earth will be cleansed and renewed by fire and final judgment will fall on all who reject Christ.

Then comes the new heavens and earth, along with the heavenly city. Finally God will live physically and forever with His people on earth. So will I get to touch God?

Thomas was told by Jesus to touch the scars in His resurrection body. We are not told if Thomas actually did touch Jesus but it sure helped him believe. During His ministry Jesus often touched people in order to heal them. At the last supper he even held and washed His disciples feet. Daniel was touched by God (Dan 8:8; 10:10) and so was John during his visit to heaven's throne (Rev. 1:17).

Yes, you will get to touch God. Touch is a great communicator of love and encouragement. God will still individually encourage you with His touch in heaven. Given the mid-east culture of Jesus' day, Jesus and His disciples would certainly have been physically demonstrative.

What an incredible thought? You will shake the hand of God one day. He will still be your sovereign so you would not presume to cling to Him. But He may well give you a hug of welcome in heaven.

Angels in heaven hold personal discussions with God (1 Kgs. 22:19-23). God values their opinion. If the angels talk to God in this way then you will even more so. He will treat you like family. Jesus is Lord but He is also our brother and friend. He is also omnipresent so you can talk with Him at anytime.

Another awesome prospect awaits you then in heaven. You will be able to personally talk to God. Of course you have a taste of that right now. By faith you can talk with God in prayer, anytime, anywhere. You can spiritually enter the very throne room through prayer and know you will be heard. But there in heaven it will be much more like your daily conversations with friends now. Physically, verbally, audibly, face to face discussions with God will be one of the highlights of heaven.

But how can He do this with everyone? He is God! Heaven is also in a spiritual dimension as well as a physical one. At the very least there is plenty of time in eternity for God to talk to everyone individually. Here's where faith in the promises of God's word override the limits of our present finite understanding. But why would God want to talk to me?

Jesus loves you, the Bible declares, and when you love someone you want to talk to them all the time. He endured the cross for the joy set before Him (Heb.12:2). Not just the joy of receiving glory from the Father but the joy of being able to share that glory forever with His children, you and me. Remember God created you for this very purpose in the first place.

If God talked with Adam in the garden, why wouldn't He long to talk to all of Adam's descendants? The human race is all one family to God. The sad part for God is He can only have fellowship in eternity with those who have been redeemed.

Will God Know My Name?

"Accepted in the beloved" Paul describes the redeemed. If you are a believer you have been chosen, adopted, and accepted by Christ (Eph. 1:4-7). You are part of God's family and Christ will treat you as such. You are very special to Him. He even knows your name.

We have already talked about the new, special name Jesus has picked out for you in heaven. So of course He will want to talk to you there. The Queen of England doesn't know my name, unless she happened to read the school roster, and she wouldn't recognize me if I met her again. Incredibly the sovereign of the universe does and will!

What an amazing thought? God wants to meet you face to face one day as much as you want to see Him. What an awesome God we serve?

Doors are kept perpetually open in the heavenly city, at least the main gates are (Rev. 21:25). There will always be free physical access to New Jerusalem, to the throne room and to God Himself. There has always been free spiritual access to God for the believer. This continues in heaven. Christ has made us kings and priests unto God (Rev. 1:6). As priests we now have the right to enter God's presence. As Kings we enjoy the privilege of reigning with Him in His kingdom and of approaching His throne at any time.

There will be no restrictions, or special privileges as far as seeing God is concerned. We are all His children in heaven. Though some, such as the tribulation martyrs, may spend more time in the throne room than on the new earth (Rev. 7:14-15), no one will be denied access to God. You can get to see Him whenever you wish.

"Dad" is how Jesus taught His disciples to address God (Matt. 6:9). This is what your relationship to God will be like in heaven. Jesus is our friend. Whoever does the will of God is Christ's brother, sister, mother (Matt. 12:50). In heaven you will do the will of God. Your relationship to Him will be as family.

As in human families now (at least according to Biblical principles), father is also to be respected and even feared as head of the home. Similarly your relationship to God will be one of love, respect and awe. You will never presume on His love. His is your sovereign Lord as well as your dad.

Those of you who had wise, godly fathers will have no problem understanding this kind of relationship our heavenly Father will have with us in heaven. For those of you who were not so fortunate, try to think of a man of God you know, admire and respect. Then try to picture them in a warm, loving, very approachable, parent role. This image will be a taste of what your relationship to God will be like in heaven.

How will I know what to say to God? How am I supposed to act in the presence of the King of Kings? Won't I be petrified? No! No more than a child greeting his father coming home from work.

Children of God, the Holy Spirit assures us to be (Rom. 8: 16,17). If we are children then we are also heirs. This is how God will treat us, as heirs of all the glory He has given His Son. No loving earthly father would ignore his heirs or have any trouble communicating with them.

This is why understanding God as your heavenly Father is so critical to understanding how you will be treated in heaven. God will make you feel completely at home in His presence, physically in heaven. Learning to be at home in His presence now, spiritually, through faith, prayer and obedience to His word is good preparation for eternity. These things develop holiness, without which no one will see the Lord (Heb. 12:14).

How and Where Will I See Jesus?

Daily you will feed on the words of God and drink of the refreshment of the Holy Spirit to sustain your spirit in heaven. This will happen primarily in the throne room of Zion, New Jerusalem. There you will worship the Lamb of God on the throne. There you will communicate with God the Father. There too you will continue to learn how to worship Him and how to approach Him.

Much of this we have covered in previous chapters in different contexts. I hope it will help solidify in your mind what heaven is like. Suffice to say here, it is in this throne room we treat our heavenly Father with the respect, awe and holy fear He deserves. It will be primarily on the new earth that we get to treat Christ as brother and friend, though always with respect.

Resurrection, bodily from the grave and His promised return assures us we will get to see Jesus, physically on the new earth. The new earth is part of His kingdom He will rule forever. We, the saints of God, will help Him rule there and enjoy familial, physical fellowship with Him.

Here on the glorious new earth you will get to walk, work and talk with Jesus. Serving Him here will be an exciting, daily, joyful experience. Truly it will be heaven on earth! All those questions you'd love to ask Him? You'll be able to get them answered personally, face to face. All those Bible messages you wished you could have heard Him preach? You will one day, on the new earth. All those things you wish you understood better? You will, as you get to know Jesus more and more each day of eternity.

Which poses the question, "will there be any need of the Bible in heaven?" After all the very Word of God Himself will be with us teaching us everything we need to know. Truth is part of the nature of God. Jesus is the truth. Preservation of recorded truth (the written revelation of Jesus Christ) is forever preserved in heaven the Bible declares (Psa. 119:89; 1 Pet. 1:25). Though Jesus is the Word, we will still have the written Word of God in heaven.

151

Jesus is the Bread of Life and the Living Water yet there is physical bread and water in heaven too which we are required to eat and drink. The Bible will still be there for you to read and understand, more and more. I believe it will still be our manual for living in heaven just as it is supposed to be for life here on earth. You will spend eternity finding out God. The Bible is the complete revelation of God. You will spend eternity finding out the depths of truths contained in His revelation.

When Jesus is not personally and physically present with you, you will have always have His written word available. Preachers may well get to continue preaching in heaven, not to save people but to teach them the eternal truths of God. Though you may be able to communicate instantly with Jesus in new and wonderful ways on the new earth, physically He can only be in one place at a time. How often you meet with Him personally may depend on what He has assigned for you to do. Of course you will never be refused an audience with Him. It just may take a while to arrange. But then you will have all the time in the world, in eternity!

Will Jesus ever come to dinner at my home? I am sure He will. After all, he assured His disciples they would one day dine with Abraham and the prophets, and so will we.

Jesus assured His disciples they would one day sup with Him again in heaven. That goes for every believer too, not just at the first great wedding banquet but individually also. Remember the Biblical pattern and type for Christ's relationship to us is the Jewish marriage. We are collectively and individually His bride. Every groom dines with his bride in the home he has prepared for her. So too will Jesus.

Here once again the spiritual and the physical promises of heaven are fleshed out. Just as Jesus promises to come into our hearts spiritually and sup with us (Rev. 3:20), so too He will physically one day come in and sup with you in that mansion He's prepared for you on high. Entertaining Jesus. What a wonderful thought. What a beautiful hope to look forward to. Heaven is a real place. It is eating and drinking, talking and laughing, loving and being loved. It is home!

Entertaining Jesus and others in your home will be part of your service in the kingdom. Christ is still our Lord and King as well as our friend. As mentioned before many will serve Him in positions of leadership and great responsibility. Others will serve Him with their special talents and creative abilities. All of us will serve Him within our family relationships and in helping care for His creation.

Each of the tasks and assignments He gives you in heaven will at some point entail meeting with the Lord, physically. You will get to see Him often in the course of your service in the Kingdom. He will of course be present at the many feasts and celebrations that seem to be so much a part of the activities of heaven.

Yes, you will get to see God (Jesus) in all of His glory on His throne in New Jerusalem. Yes, you will get to see Jesus (God) as you serve in His Kingdom on the new earth. The Father, Son and Holy Spirit will live with us forever in heaven as head of the family of the redeemed. But what about our earthly families? Will I see my relatives in heaven? Will we live in families? What if all my relatives are unsaved? Relationships are very important in heaven so let's examine what the Bible says about them a little further.

CHAPTER 15

WHAT ABOUT MY RELATIVES?

Will I See My Loved Ones in Heaven?

Goodbyes are hard to say at the best of times. They are well nigh impossible when you know in your heart you will never see that person again.

"Make sure you bring those grandchildren to see me next time you come over and make it soon. Otherwise, my son, dad and I will be seeing you in heaven."

Dad had passed away less than a year before and mom's heart and health were failing rapidly. I had taken time off to fly to the UK and spend a couple of weeks visiting with her in the nursing home. We had been unable to go over for Dad's funeral and I wanted to make up for it.

I'm glad I did. God's timing, as ever, was perfect. Mom and I enjoyed some very special moments together, laughing about the past, getting up to date on the present, and discussing the future, yes, including heaven. She even perked up enough for my sister, Heather, and I to take her out of the nursing home a couple of times. She loved dining at nice restaurants. A few months after I returned to the USA God took her home.

"I'll try and bring the whole family over next year, mom, and if not, like you said, we'll see each other again in heaven. What a great reunion that will be."

There were no tears in her eyes, just love, as I closed the door to her bedroom for the last time. Heaven does that for you. Not just the place, so much as He who came from heaven. Riding down on the elevator I felt a great sense of peace, assurance, and even anticipation that I really will see mom again.

Christ's resurrection assures us we will see believing relatives again. David was able to get a handle on his grief when his infant son died because of his firm belief in the resurrection. "I shall go to him, but he shall not return to me," he confidently told his servants, after unsuccessfully pleading with God to let his son live (2 Sam. 12:23). Jesus promised the disciples that they would get to dine with their ancestors, Abraham, Isaac and Jacob, in heaven (Matt. 8:11).

God promised Aaron and Moses they would meet their loved ones in heaven (Nu. 27:13). The New Testament promises over and over again that all the saints of God will be there. You will get to see them and you'll never have to say goodbye again.

Resurrection of the body assures you of the joy of meeting those who have gone on before you to heaven. As discussed already you will have no problem recognizing your loved ones up there except perhaps to exclaim, "My, how good you look!" Though they will seem similar in appearance, we may have a hard time recognizing the amazing new, Christ-like character of some of our relatives (Just kidding uncle Joe!).

All the misunderstandings, hasty judgments, disappointments, resentments and hurts of the past that can happen in even the best of relationships, will be forgiven and forgotten. There will only be unconditional love and ecstatic joy at seeing each other again.

Special relationships, we have seen, will continue in heaven. So our spouses will continue to be an important part of our lives in heaven, assuming they are believers. Though Jesus taught there is no marrying in heaven, family relationships will still be acknowledged there, given some of the passages already quoted.

The Sadducees' hypothetical question to Jesus about the woman with seven husbands who dies and goes to heaven misses the whole perspective of relationships there (Matt. 22:23-33). The main point Jesus was making was the fact in eternity we will have living relationships with living people and a living God. We will all be children of God and part of one huge family in heaven. We will enjoy a spiritual intimacy of relationship with everyone there, as our brother and sister in Christ. Everyone you meet will be a close, personal relative!

This kind of "open" society is almost beyond our comprehension given our sin-filled, proud, selfish world today. Imagine being free to instantly trust, open up to, and love everyone you meet without fear of rejection? You will never feel so safe and secure as a person as you will in heaven. And this society lasts forever!

Adam was created a man, not a child. Everything in heaven is complete and mature. Though we have looked at this already it bears repeating in this section about relationships. No, I can find nothing in Scripture that indicates there will be children there. Remember heaven is forever. Would you condemn little ones to never grow up in all eternity?

Certainly, saved children go to heaven but they will be given new, adult bodies just like everyone else. Yes, God has a special love for the little ones because of their innocence and trust. Yes, they have special guardian angels to watch over them but no, they will not remain as children in heaven.

Will We Live in Families?

Marriage and family was the first social institution ordained by God in the garden of Eden. God's people Israel camped in the desert in family tribes. They settled the promised land in their family tribes. The frequent recordings of family genealogies including Christ's, throughout Scripture, remind us not only of the historical fact of the Biblical record but of the importance of the family to God.

In the New Testament, believers are spiritually adopted into God's family becoming children of God (Gal. 4:5-6). Christ called everyone who does the will of God His brother and sister (Matt. 12:50). During the Tribulation years Israel's tribal affiliations are restored (Rev. 7:4-8). Old Testament descriptions of the millennium include feasting and fellowshipping together in families.   The names of the twelve family tribes of Israel are built into the heavenly city (Rev. 21:12).

God is our Father in heaven and the saints are known as the family of God.   Given these patterns, types and principles throughout the Bible it seems evident that they continue into eternity.   Life and activities in heaven will again focus around family units, just as they have always done in God's plan and purpose so far.   Aside from the absence of little children, the biggest difference will be that every individual family unit will be intimately related to every other family unit in heaven in a way the world has not yet seen.   True fellowship within the church is a beginning taste of that experience now.

Authority, leadership, and specific roles within the church, the family of God on earth, is related to spiritual gifts and maturity and the calling of God.   Though everyone is equal in Christ, in heaven there will still be varying responsibilities and roles within the family units. Faithfulness on earth now in the roles and with the gifts God gives you (however unimportant they may seem to you), will result in the reward of greater responsibility and authority in heaven.

But don't worry, whatever your role is in heaven, your heavenly family will hold you in the highest regard and treat you with the greatest respect.   Nonetheless, now is the time to press toward the mark for the prize of the high calling of God in Christ Jesus (Phil. 3:14).

Records, detailed records, are kept in heaven on every person and family.   You will be able to accurately trace your ancestry back to Noah and Adam.   More than this, you will have the opportunity to meet and spend time with your ancestors that made it into heaven.   What a fascinating experience to hear and see first hand how God has worked down through the generations to you!

Can you imagine the incredible family get-togethers you will have in heaven and what amazing stories will be told there?   Of course the stories will all be true and not even exaggerated,   each one of them demonstrating God's loving purpose and saving grace.

Paul and John frequently addressed believers, to whom they brought the gospel, as their "little children."   These spiritual converts are the apostle's joy and crown. Timothy and Philemon and others whom Paul personally discipled are written to and treated as sons.

There is a very special relationship here on earth with those whom you personally help come to Christ and disciple in the church, your spiritual children. These special relationships continue in heaven. As crowns of joy they are part of the rewards of eternity. They will be a special part of your extended family there.

Being a crown of reward, your spiritual children would be initially identified to you at the Bema seat of Christ. Are you beginning to see some (most!) of the greatest joys and rewards of heaven are relationships? The material opulence enjoyed there is simply a fantastic fringe benefit to enhance the time spent with the people of heaven.

Weddings, like funerals, are often the only time major family reunions occur. There are no funerals in heaven but there will be one massive, magnificent wedding banquet take place. First, at the Bema ceremony you'll get to see everyone in heaven individually announced and presented to receive their rewards. Then the real reunion with the saints and loved ones begins at the marriage feast of the Lamb.

Think of the happiest, grandest wedding you've ever attended where you got to meet friends you hadn't seen for ages and you laughed and talked for hours after the ceremony. This would be a mere hint, a minute taste of what the wedding in heaven will be like. Joy and excitement unspeakable! If you trust in Christ you already have an invite!

Do My Loved Ones in Heaven See Me Now?

Martyrs of the great Tribulation are aware of what is happening on earth, while in their intermediate state awaiting the end of the age (Rev. 6:9,10). But as already discussed from Luke 16, the saints in heaven cannot communicate with those still on earth. So I doubt very much if your loved ones in heaven can actually see what you are doing now. At least there is no direct Biblical evidence of this happening.

Despite the many stories, songs and movies written about grandpa looking down from heaven and watching his grandson make the winning touch-down, it is more emotion than Biblical reality. Oh, I understand and identify with those feelings. Both my parents died before I finished my PhD. I like to think they rejoiced in heaven when I finally walked the stage at graduation. I am sure they did but not because they were actually watching me.

You see, in the intermediate state in heaven they have only temporary spiritual form. They have not yet received their new physical bodies. They cannot yet move from the spiritual to the physical and back again or even leave heaven and come to the spiritual realm around earth as the angels do. Christ keeps them close to Himself in paradise in the heavenly city while they patiently wait for His return to earth and their final transformation. The only two exceptions to this are Moses and Elijah at the Transfiguration, and the resurrected saints at Christ's resurrection (Matt. 27:52,53).

Revelation does indicate, however, that those in heaven are made aware of what's happening, generally on earth. This probably comes from the Holy Spirit, angel reports, and from Christ Himself. Remember Christ is interceding daily for you before the Father in heaven. The saints there are kept up to date on what the spirit of Christ is accomplishing in the lives of His children on earth. They are longing for Him to complete His purposes on earth in you and in history and usher in His kingdom.

Until that day, when Christ returns to earth for His own, the saints in heaven are kept from all the problems and worries of earth. They are continually at peace with Him, joyfully awaiting the climax of the age.

Will I Know or Care if Some of My Relatives Are Not in Heaven?

Sorrow and regret continue to exist in hell but not in heaven, at least not in the way we sorrow now. There will be no more tears there (Rev. 21:4). Furthermore, God's perfect justice will be more fully understood and appreciated by us when we get to heaven. So if you discover certain of your relatives are not there, somehow it will not distress you. If this seems hard to take. If you have some dear, gentle, good-living loved one that hasn't seen their need of Christ yet, then keep on praying.

God does not wish anyone to perish and go to hell (2 Pet. 3:9). While they are still alive there is still hope. But ultimately the choice is theirs. God never forces anyone to accept Him.

So what about my relatives that have already died? Will I see them in heaven? Only the Lord really knows the answer to that one. Only He sees into their hearts. Only He knows if perhaps they turned to Him in their last moments as the reality of their own mortality took hold. Only He knows how much of the gospel they ever really heard or understood. But what if they were obviously evil, ungodly individuals? Once again you just have to trust in the mercy, grace and justice of God.

God takes no pleasure in the death of the wicked yet His holiness demands He judge sin and sinners. At the Great White Throne judgment you will experience only a great satisfaction at the justice of God in dealing with even your own relatives that reject His salvation. You will see and hear just how wicked they really were.

How can this be? I thought heaven was a place of love for all men? Yes, but it is also a place of perfect Holiness. Even the martyrs in heaven cry out to God to avenge their blood on those who killed them (Rev. 6:10). They appeal to His justice and holiness. There is no mercy and love without righteousness. But yes, in heaven you will also be amazed at the grace of God when you see certain relatives there you never thought would make it!

What the Bible is trying to tell you in all of this is you will see things, people and events from a whole different perspective when you get to heaven. You will see them from God's perspective.

All of us get upset when the news media reports only half a story, slanting it towards their own particular point of view. We hate political spin-doctoring that doesn't deliberately lie but doesn't tell the whole truth either. Yet to be fair to the press and politicians, sometimes they just don't know all the facts, or they don't get them straight. But God knows every fact about everything and everyone, and He cannot lie. That's why Jesus *is* the truth. This is why in heaven, as His children, we will finally understand even the seemingly "unfair" things of life. We will know and applaud the truth . . . even about our loved ones!

Reunions are great if you happen to know most of the people who are there. If you don't, it can be a very lonely experience. So what if I don't have any living relatives or I'm not even sure who my close relatives are? Will I be lonely and unhappy at the wedding feast in heaven? Of course not. There are no lonely people in heaven. You will be pleasantly surprised to discover there are countless individuals related to you in heaven, both physically and spiritually.

Most of all you will meet your heavenly Father who loves you more than any earthly relative ever could. God is a father of the fatherless, He setteth the solitary in families (Psa. 68:5,6). Anyway, in heaven everyone will be your brother or sister and they will all treat you as such even if you were not related on earth. The concept and name of the family is derived from the fellowship of the Godhead (Eph. 3:14,15). You will be part of a very special family in heaven. In Christ, you are already part of that family now.

Family is much more than just a blood relationship, anyway. Every happily adopted child understands this. They know they are special because they have been chosen. Christ has chosen the redeemed to be His adopted children (Eph. 1:4,5; Gal. 4:4-6). Every true believer is a son or daughter and heir of Christ. It is the children of faith, Jew or Gentile, who are the true children of Abraham and heirs to God's promises (Rom.9) .

God keeps careful track of both blood and adoptive relatives. If they are believers they all will become an important part of your family life in heaven. His plans and purposes for our lives are always perfect. He doesn't make mistakes. We will finally understand all this when we meet in heaven. In fact part of the joy of eternity will be developing and deepening our relationships, beginning with those we had on earth and extending to the whole family of God.

For those of you who are part of a warm loving family with lots of friendly relatives and extended family, you already have a taste of the relationships in heaven. For those who have not been blessed with a happy, loving, extended family on earth, God is already preparing one for you in eternity. Get yourself involved with a local body of believers, and hopefully you'll begin to experience a taste of those heavenly relationships now.

Speaking of extended family what about racial differences. Will we all be one color, culture, and people in heaven? Will there be nations, taxation and representation in the Kingdom of God? What exactly will Kingdom living be like? Indeed, why is heaven referred to as a Kingdom? This is what we will examine next as we continue to look at the relationships of heaven.

CHAPTER 16

KINGDOM LIVING

Will There Be Racial Distinctions in Heaven?

"Pastor, who was that family in church last Sunday, the one with all the black kids?"

"Black kids?"

I racked my brains trying to think of any black children in our church. It was a very white rural community we lived in.

"You know, they sat on the right near the back. There must have been at least twenty of them!"

This was a slight exaggeration but now I knew who he meant and I was beginning to get angry at the obvious distaste in his voice. I told him so, in no uncertain terms. He was a little taken aback.

"Those children are some of the most precious and well behaved in the church. If you had just mentioned one of their names I would have instantly known which family you were referring to."

Like everyone else in the church, I had grown to know and love them by personality, not color. I really had to think hard when he first asked me the question. Actually, this caring family included

165

black, white, and Hispanic children. But then prejudiced people are rarely observant!

There's no room for bigotry in the family of God, on earth or in heaven. Everyone is equal in Christ, Jew and Greek, male and female (Rom.11:12; Col 3:11,28). Jesus broke all the social mores in this area. He reached out in love to Gentiles and Jews, the hated Samaritans, Roman soldiers, beggars, lepers, scholars, and the rich and powerful. He publicly elevated women, and His disciples ran the gambit from fisherman to physician. It will not matter who or what you are or were, or where you came from, in the kingdom of heaven. In fact cultural differences will be specially honored in Christ's kingdom.

Kings (plural) of the earth bring their cultural glory to New Jerusalem (Rev. 21:24). Saved *nations* (plural) walk in the light of this city. *Israel* and its 12 tribes are a recognized part of this heavenly metropolis. National distinctions are maintained in heaven.

Yes, but couldn't this just mean people from every nation of the old earth? John sees a multitude of all nations, kindred, people and tongues in heaven (Rev. 7:9). They are all dressed in similar white robes, all part of Christ's church. Yet John recognizes and records their varied cultural differences including their languages, which are still evident even though they are now in heaven.

You could argue these are still in their intermediate state, in this passage, but not so the nations and kings of Revelation 21! Once again John uses Old Testament imagery here. Isaiah predicts the future glory of both millennial Jerusalem and the eternal city of Zion (Isa. 60). He speaks of the kings and nations of earth bringing their wealth and homage to both cities. How do I know Isaiah is referring also to heaven and not just the millennial kingdom?

Verse 19 of Isaiah 60 speaks of a city that doesn't need the sun because the Lord will be its light (cf Rev. 22:5). Only the eternal city, not the millennial Jerusalem, fits this description. Notice also where John (Rev.21:25) gets his picture of the New Jerusalem gates being perpetually open (Isa. 60:11). The last chapter of Isaiah (66) is a description of the return of Israel to Jerusalem, the

166

end of the Tribulation, and the setting up of Christ's millennial kingdom on this earth. Yet God himself (Isa. 66:22) parallels it all with the new heavens and new earth. He promises that the seed and name (national distinction) of Israel will remain forever. Notice also the reference to nations in the rest of the chapter.

Just as there are nations in the millennium so there will be nations in eternity. We are all part of the human race. We all came from Adam. Individual races and separate cultures began after man's rebellion at the tower of Babel (Gen. 11:9). Evidently, in the wisdom and grace of God, these racial differences collectively reflect the glory of God, rather than man's rebellion, and will continue to do so in the kingdom of heaven.

Of course, like today, the separate nations of heaven may well include multiple races. Many individuals today have multiple ethnic backgrounds. But don't worry, God knows exactly which country you would be happiest to be a part of in heaven.

Why Is Heaven Called a Kingdom?

Kingdom implies one-person sovereignty. A sovereign rules over subjects. The kingdom of heaven is called such because it is the ultimate, eternal kingdom with the ultimate, eternal sovereign, Jesus Christ. We are all subjects of God's kingdom (Psa. 103:19). We are all His creatures, made in His image.

Because of sin, however, we are not all automatically subjects of heaven. The kingdom Jesus tells His disciples to pray for (Matt. 6:10), is not the same kingdom as the Psalmist writes about. This kingdom Jesus was talking about is future, the physical millennial kingdom and heaven itself. It is also a present kingdom, a spiritual kingdom. Kingdoms provide protection and privileges to obedient, submissive subjects. Those who by faith submit their lives to the total sovereignty of Christ become part of this kingdom of heaven right now! Wherever Christ is, ruling in the hearts of His people, there is the kingdom of heaven.

Heaven therefore is no political democracy, it is a monarchy or more specifically, a theocracy, for the king of heaven is God. It is the future, physical, eternal kingdom of heaven that this book is concerned with. The terms *kingdom of heaven* and *kingdom of*

God refer essentially to the same thing in Scripture. In addition there are several types of kingdoms in the Bible which can make it all a little confusing. So I will first try to define *kingdom* for you and then look in more detail into the final kingdom of heaven, eternity.

Kingdoms have three main aspects. First, they have a monarch, a king who has final and absolute authority. Second, kingdoms have territory or a realm, lands that the king rules over and the kingdom's subjects live and work in. Third they have governance, the active reign of a sovereign, who, with the help of his leaders, makes sure the laws of the kingdom are obeyed and the people protected and provide for.

Heaven has a monarch, territory, and governance. Heaven is a kingdom ruled by God, in the sovereign person of Christ. The realm of eternity includes New Jerusalem, the new earth, a new universe and of course the redeemed saints of God. The kingdom of heaven is governed by Christ from the throne of heaven, located in the New Jerusalem. Everything the subjects of heaven need is already provided for them forever. Heaven is a kingdom that never ends.

Because heaven is a kingdom there is no majority rule. It is not run by public opinion or personal emotion. Its subjects live by truth. Heaven's sovereign *is* the truth! So anything He says goes. Everything He (Christ) says is perfect and good. Everyone in His kingdom really does live happily ever after. *Joyfully* ever after would be a better description. In heaven our satisfaction will not depend on happenings (circumstances), though these will be awesome. The joy and satisfaction of heaven comes from the relationship each subject has with heaven's king, Jesus.

Israel was a type of the physical kingdom of God on earth, reaching its zenith in the reigns of David and Solomon. The longed for millennial reign of Israel, a predicted one thousand year rule under Christ, will be a physical kingdom of God on this earth. Heaven, when God dwells forever with man, will become the final and permanent physical kingdom of God on the new earth.

These are the major physical kingdoms of God. Of course all creation is His physical kingdom too. If Adam had not sinned then this earth would have become the eternal kingdom of heaven. If Israel had been able to keep the Law (a theological impossibility) they would have become a living demonstration of what the kingdom of heaven was like.

When Christ returns to earth to set up His millennial reign, Israel (the saved remnant) will indeed demonstrate to the whole world the kingdom of heaven on earth. There will be peace and justice and perfect government for the first time on this earth. The Jews will regain all the land promised to them by God's covenant. Their city of Jerusalem will become the capital of the world. Christ will rule the nations from here with the help of His saints.

This old world will have peace one day. It will be ruled by a king, the Prince of Peace, Jesus. This kingdom will last for a thousand years.

Israel, with its faithful prophets, priests, patriarchs, kings and believing remnant is a picture of the spiritual kingdom of God. The gentile church, founded upon Jewish apostles, Jewish scriptures, and a Jewish Messiah, currently represents the spiritual kingdom of heaven on earth. Of course many Christian Jews, are part and parcel of this too.

As already mentioned, the spiritual kingdom of God exists in the hearts of all true believers everywhere. In this sense the kingdom of heaven is within you, as well as all around you spiritually. In the latter sense, the angels are part of this spiritual dimension of the kingdom of heaven. Whenever a person receives Christ by faith, they enter the spiritual kingdom of heaven. Whenever you pray or worship God in spirit and in truth, you enter this spiritual kingdom of heaven. You can't see it (yet!) with your physical eyes, only the eyes of faith. But it's there and it's real. When just two or three gather in Christ's name He is right there!

Since creation there has always been this two-fold aspect to the kingdom of heaven, physical and spiritual. It existed in the mind and purpose of God even before the foundation of the world. The eternal throne of God in the spiritual realm of heaven has physical aspects to it, including now the physical presence of Christ. The physical and spiritual heaven of eternity is already prepared and waiting for you.

What Forerunners of the Kingdom Are There?

Creation of the universe and this world before the fall was a forerunner and type of this kingdom of heaven to come. To recap then, Eden, Israel, the promised land, the church, the millennial kingdom are all forerunners of this kingdom God has planned for us. They are each types of heaven, both spiritually and physically. The more you know and understand God's purpose in each of these, the more you will be able to understand the kingdom of heaven.

The problem is man distorts the true image of heaven in each of these types. God's ultimate purposes are not thwarted but our understanding of heaven is dimmed. Adam disobeyed God in Eden. Israel became apostate, rejecting God and His Messiah. The promised land was never fully conquered allowing idolatry to assimilate the true worship of Jehovah. So God's people never experienced the promised rest from their enemies.

The visible Church will eventually become a luke-warm, apostate, one-world religion, assimilating the Laodicean culture of the end-times (Rev. 3:15,16). Whole nations rebel against Christ's rule at the conclusion of the millennium. Nonetheless, each of these types give you a picture or taste of what the kingdom of heaven is going to be like.

Jesus presented many pictures of heaven in His sermons. The kingdom of heaven must be a priority in life (Matt.6:19-21;33). The kingdom of heaven is very precious. It is worth more than buried treasure or priceless gem-stones (Matt. 13:44-46).

Matthew's Gospel records the word for heaven 82 times, even more than John uses it in Revelation (57 times). Most of these occurrences in Matthew are from the mouth of Jesus. The majority of these are in the phrase, "kingdom of heaven." Clearly our Lord wanted the people, and His disciples in particular, to know what the kingdom of heaven would be like. He wanted them to have a hope, an excitement, a desire to be a part of His coming kingdom, both the millennium (for His Jewish listeners in particular) and the heaven of eternity.

Mysteries of the kingdom of heaven are revealed in the parables of Jesus (Matt. 13:11). The parable of the laborers and the parable of the talents, for example, reveal much about status, rewards, and responsibilities in heaven. Other parables, such as the sower, wheat and tares, and two sons, indicate what kind of people will be there. Parables such as the leaven, fish net, and mustard seed, speak of entrance into and growth of the kingdom here and now. All the parables point to the spiritual kingdom of God's people, to the physical kingdom of the millennium, and also to the eternal kingdom of heaven.

Christ's teaching in the beatitudes point not only to ethical principles for living in the millennium, but also to spiritual principles of life in eternity. His kingdom lasts forever. It is eternal. Thus any and all kingdoms of God, both spiritual and physical, prior to the final state of the redeemed is a picture, type and pattern in some aspect of what is to come. Jesus consistently calls it the kingdom of *heaven*, in His teachings in the gospels. Heaven is forever no matter how you interpret the context.

How Will the Kingdom Be Ruled?

Kingdoms of this world will one day become the kingdoms of Christ who will reign over them forever and ever (Rev. 11:15). The saints and servants of God will reign with Christ on the new earth (Rev. 5:10), and help Him reign from New Jerusalem forever (Rev. 22:5). The rule of heaven will be characterized by righteousness (Isa. 32:1).

Note the fact Christ will reign over the nations *forever*, not just in the millennium. Here again Scripture points to the fact of similar nations, countries and cultures of this present earth being there in eternity. The saints helping Christ rule His kingdom forever includes reigning with Him on this earth during the millennium (Rev. 20:6). The saints are appointed as priests and kings in the kingdom of heaven. Clearly there will be individual nations to rule within the realm of heaven's kingdom.

Not only does the Bible characterize the kingdom of heaven by righteousness but also by joy. The Lord's rule over the world and creation causes the people and the earth to rejoice (Psa. 97:1; see also Psalm 98). Life in the kingdom of heaven will be full of joy and celebration. Can you imagine living in a society where

171

everyone is so happy with leadership decisions, they rejoice and celebrate? Can you imagine a world where no one ever again complains about government? Yes, it's possible! It's predicted. It's prepared. It's the kingdom of heaven. And it's real! See you there?

National distinctions of culture, dress and language will be controlled and developed by the national leaders Christ appoints on the new earth. John and the Old Testament prophets paint a picture of the kings of the new earth bringing the cultural glories of their nations as gifts to Christ in New Jerusalem. It is a fascinating prediction of the continuance of national pride in our cultural distinctions. All the things you love about your own particular race and country (that are honoring to God) will be there in heaven and will continue to be developed in bringing ongoing glory to God.

Racial distinctions will become something to be prized, shared, and rejoiced over by everyone. It will bring the peoples of the world together in celebration rather than dividing them. Man's marred attempts at this such as the Olympics and the Year 2000 celebrations give us a minute taste of what the kingdom of heaven will be like. Of course much of national culture is influenced by religious belief systems. In heaven every nation will worship the king of heaven, Jesus Christ, and Him alone (Phil. 2:9-11).

Revelation speaks of the nations of them that are saved (Rev. 21:24). If this refers to the nations collectively and not just to individuals from those nations then some countries we know now may not be in heaven. The land promises in God's covenant with Israel assures this nation of distinct areas and boundaries on the new earth forever. Other nations God allows into heaven will have their own territories to rule over.

Every nation, however, will be part of one kingdom, a kind of united nations of heaven, ruled over by Christ. Gog and Magog (parts of modern Russia) who rebel at the end of the millennial rule, may not be in heaven. Other nations that rebel against Christ and the rule of Israel may well be missing too. How God decides to divide up the new earth into countries remains to be seen. Rest assured the makeup of the kingdom of heaven will be just and perfect. You will be more than satisfied with the make-up of the nations in heaven.

Who Will Govern the Nations in Heaven?

Faithful stewards of time, money and talent on earth will become the rulers of the nations in heaven. The humblest servants of Christ here will hold the highest positions in the kingdom. The spiritually mature and those who have faithfully lived and taught the word of God on earth will govern and judge in heaven. These are the principles Jesus taught in the parables and the Sermon on the Mount.

Now you can begin to see why no one will want or need to complain about the government in heaven. The rulers in the kingdom will be the humblest, smartest, most Christ-like, and kindest people you could hope to meet. The Bible talks about rulers of cities, about kings and priests, about servants and families, all being part of eternity. These authority systems, God's chain of command if you like, will continue in heaven. They will all work in beautiful harmony together bringing glory to God and peace to man, under the leadership of Christ.

Instant communication will remove all fear of misunderstandings or misrepresentation before the rulers of heaven. Besides, every individual will always have an advocate in Christ and direct access to Him. There will be no taxes, liens or loans in heaven! Everyone's property will be owned, free and clear forever. Possessions will be freely shared so no one will ever be in need.

There will be nothing to hinder, restrict, frustrate or stifle your hopes and dreams in heaven. Everything the Lord sets your hearts to do you will accomplish. Life will be a beach! Forever and ever!

"Prince of Peace," Isaiah calls the Messiah, "Of the increase of His government and peace there shall be no end (Isa. 9:6,7).

The Lord will bless His people with peace (Psa. 29:10,11). Our redemption in Christ makes us at peace *with* God now. The Holy

Spirit brings us the peace *of* God, in our hearts. In heaven's perfect kingdom you will physically, spiritually and emotionally enjoy the peace of God, and peace with God, forever and ever.

Peace, perfect peace, this is the true *rest* of heaven. Everyone will be at peace in the kingdom of heaven. Families, workers, leaders, towns, cities, governments, nations, will work together in harmony and peace, all the time! Sounds like an impossible dream? God has promised it. By faith you can begin to live it now, through Christ who is your peace. In heaven the whole universe will be at peace, forever and ever. Don't you long to be there? It makes the Lord's prayer a whole lot more meaningful.

"Thy kingdom come."

We have said the angels are part of the spiritual kingdom of heaven. If angels are spirit beings without a permanent physical body what relationship, if any, will we have with them in heaven? What are angels really like, what is their function? How are they organized? How many are there? Why did God create them?

CHAPTER 17

TOUCHED BY ANGELS

Will There Be Angels in Heaven?

Powerful forces tugged at my steering wheel as we careened back and forth across the multiple lanes of the toll-way. We'd broad-sided the near-side crash-barrier at 70 miles an hour and now were in an uncontrollable skid. I was afraid to touch the brakes in case we spun around completely and flipped over. Every time we skidded into the middle lane a white Cadillac came within inches of our fender, its driver blissfully unaware of our close encounters.

A wasp had zoomed in through an open window. In momentary panic I took my eyes off the road. My alert wife flicked the insect out of the window with the road map. She also happened to throw out the money for the next toll booth! But this was the least of my worries.

In those few seconds the road banked sharply to the left. We were heading straight for a steel and concrete barrier. I yanked the wheel over managing to hit the barrier sideways instead of head-on. There was noise of screaming metal and I was sure the car was being demolished. The impact catapulted us back onto the highway.

It took almost two miles to steer out of the skid and come to a halt on the shoulder. I am convinced to this day that someone else was doing the steering. My efforts to control the car were futile. The wheel just didn't respond. Yet we were all unharmed and the vehicle suffered only a long dent, a few scratches and a jammed window. We walked back shakily to the curve in the road where we'd hit. There was a 60-foot drop into a ravine the other side of the barrier! Surely, guardian angels were watching out for us that day?

The Bible says angels do exist and they do indeed watch out for God's people on earth. They are also very much part of the kingdom of heaven. So why don't we see them and what are they really like?

Angels are spirits (Heb. 1:14), who can appear in human form (Heb. 13:1), but their bodies are not like ours. They do not have physical flesh and bones (Luke 24:37-39). In heaven the angels are seen to have wings, the Seraphim having six wings and the Cherubim four wings. They are very powerful (Psa. 103:19) and currently excel man in their knowledge. Sometimes they appear on earth as men, such as the angels that visited Sodom. At other times they appear to men as bright and fearful angels of God.

Though they are rarely seen in visible form today they are still active in the affairs of this world and the church (Eph. 3;10). Jesus himself appeared in angel form on earth, prior to His incarnation. On these occasions the Bible refers to Him as the angel of the Lord. The Book of Hebrews makes it clear, however, that Jesus is not an angel. He is far superior to any angel. Christ was never created. He is God. He willingly became a little lower than the angels for our sakes while on earth. But after the cross and resurrection He received back all the glory that was His before, as the eternal Son of God. Unlike the angels He now possesses a permanent physical, glorified body.

Thirty four books of the Bible give reference to angels. They are mentioned over 270 times in Scripture. They do not marry or reproduce and were created at the beginning of creation in huge numbers (Psa. 148:2-5). From the creation of the earth to its final judgment angels are very much a part of the scene in heaven. Those angels who did not follow Satan in his rebellion will continue to be an essential part of eternity.

Though angels are powerful creatures they are not omnipotent (all powerful) or omniscient (all knowing) or even omnipresent. They have emotions and a will but are not heirs of God, nor can they testify to the grace of God in salvation. Unlike mankind, Scripture never mentions angels singing, only speaking and crying out.

How Are the Angels Organized?

Archangels are the highest ranking. The only Archangel named in Scripture is Michael (Jude 9). Next in rank come the Seraphim (Isa.6; Rev. 4), strange and beautiful creatures that serve God above and beside His throne. Cherubim (Ezek.chap.1 & 10), are similar creatures, which serve God beneath His throne. Satan, as Lucifer, was once chief of the Cherubim (Ezek. 28:13-15). The angels are highly organized beings and their hierarchy includes spiritual principalities and powers (Rom. 8:37; Col. 1:16).

Gabriel, one of the only two named angels, appeared to Daniel, Zechariah (John the-Baptist's father), and Mary. Even though he brought the greatest message ever to earth, the birth of Messiah, Gabriel is not named as an archangel. Michael's primary responsibility on earth is the protection of Israel (Dan. 10:13,21). Seraphim's main ministry is to praise the name of God in the throne room and teach others to worship Him. The Cherubim guard the throne area of God and are surrounded in mystery. These are the creatures which Ezekiel saw moving around heaven in strange wheeled machines. Millions of other angels make up the host of heaven, worshipping and serving God and His saints.

Throne room appearances of the angels are throughout Scripture in both Old and New Testaments. Here is where the good angels of God, the heavenly host, reside. They have access to the second heaven, the spirit realm around the earth. It is here they do battle with the fallen angels (demons) and Satan. From time to time they appear visibly to men on earth.

The Old Testament speaks of the host of heaven (the angels) surrounding God's throne (1 Chron. 22:19; Neh. 9:6). This host is often described as the armies of heaven (Dan 4). In the New Testament the angels are seen to be in heaven's throne room also. John sees the angels who bring God's judgments on earth as proceeding out of the throne to the spiritual realm around the earth (Rev. 16:1,2; 18:1).

177

The fallen angels dwell in hell (the pit or abyss) along with Satan, situated beneath the earth. Many of them are permanently bound in chains and darkness to await the judgment (Jude 6). The rest assist Satan in ruling the affairs of the unredeemed on earth. These are like wandering spirits looking and longing for something to inhabit and control, like the evil spirits Jesus cast out of the Gaderene demoniac. They begged Christ to let them inhabit something (the pigs) and not be sent back to the abyss (Luke 8:30-33).

Why Did God Create Angels?

Praising God, serving Him and His creation, including mankind, declaring His word, doing His work and forever beholding His face. This is what God created angels to be, His holy messengers. Both in Hebrew (*malak*), and in Greek (*angelos*), the word for angel has the basic meaning of messenger. They are personal beings (Psa. 8:4,5) yet not made in God's image quite as man is. Christ did not die for angels only for men. The angels who rebelled were forever condemned and given no opportunity for redemption.

Most of us would love to see an angel. They are indeed beautiful and powerful spirit beings. Though they talk to God, freely around the throne, they are forever His messengers not His heirs as the redeemed are. Man was created to have unique fellowship with God. Angels were created to serve Him.

They serve God in multiple ways, carrying out His judgments, and His blessing upon earth. They can control the weather for God's purposes. They can influence political leaders and whole armies for God and one day will even preach the gospel, towards the end of the Tribulation. Indeed, they already announced such to the shepherds, 2000 years ago. They are a vital part of the administration of heaven now. They will continue to be so in eternity.

Hosts of heaven can refer in context to stars as well as angels. Both kind of hosts are described as beyond counting (Heb. 12:22). There are myriad angels. Jesus spoke of thousands of angels at His disposal (Matt. 26:53). John sees millions upon millions of them

178

in heaven (Rev. 5:11). In the Old Testament the angel armies of God seen by Elijah, Joshua and several other Biblical leaders are always seen in vast numbers.

The primary Hebrew words translated as *host* refer to a mass of people or a huge encampment, such as an army. In fact the appearance of multiple angels consistently indicates a fighting force. The angels are God's spiritual soldiers as well as His servants.

One third of the angel population of heaven rebelled against God including Satan. These fallen angels became the demons that were cast down to the spiritual realm of earth. Under Satan's leadership they temporarily control the kingdoms of the world. The angels in heaven are sent to minister to God's people. This is why they constantly do battle with the demons to protect God's people on earth from Satan's schemes. Fortunately the angels out-number the demons two to one!

Millions of angels join the saints in heaven praising God before His throne. The hosts of heaven in the New Testament appear more often as a mass of heavenly heralds than as a battling army. From the announcement of the Savior's birth to the worship scene in the throne room to the pouring out God's judgments on earth, they are seen in their primary role as messengers rather than soldiers.

The heaven of eternity will be filled with countless angels. Millions upon millions of them will be at the disposal of Christ and His saints. Angels guard the gates of the heavenly city, and angel guides took John on his tour of this fabulous place. From the gates to the throne room the angels are everywhere and will continue to be in eternity. Our existence in heaven will constantly be touched by angels.

Announcing what God is about to accomplish on earth is a major function of the angels which John records for us. Participating and leading in worship is a another function of the myriad hosts of heaven. Serving Christ and the redeemed of heaven is a third major activity of these wonderful beings. The glorious angels of God will continue these functions throughout eternity.

No longer will they have to announce God's judgments. In eternity they will joyfully announce Christ's ongoing plans for His kingdom. They will help keep the earth up to date, as it were, with all the announcements from the throne room. You will hear angels and see angels all the time in heaven, whether you are working on the new earth or worshipping in New Jerusalem. They will never be in your way though. Like a trusted servant and friend the angels will simply be there when you need them.

What Happens to the Fallen Angels?

Hell was prepared for Satan and his angels, (Matt. 25:41). After the Great White Throne judgment this place, along with Satan, his angels, and unredeemed mankind is thrown into the Lake of Fire for all eternity (Rev. 20:13-15). There will be no fallen angels therefore in heaven. Now known as demons, these rebellious spirit beings will never again behold the face of God. Which means you will never again be conscious of their existence and the angels of God will never again have to do battle with them.

Have you ever considered the fallen angels are the ultimate example of the effect of being away from God's presence? When they were cast out of heaven (Jude 6), they were no longer bright and beautiful spirit beings. Dwelling in darkness instead of light they became demons, hideous spirit beings using their great powers to seek and destroy God, His angels, His children, and all that is good. Satan, himself once was the brightest and most beautiful of the angels. As Lucifer he was known as the Daystar (Isa. 14:12) a title similar to Christ's. Now he is known only as a repulsive reptile, the dragon or serpent, and the father of lies, the great deceiver.

Fortunately for us, Satan and his minions will have no part in the heaven of eternity.

Are There Really Guardian Angels?

Lazarus the beggar, Jesus tells us, was taken to heaven by the angels (Luke 16:22). Elijah was apparently accompanied by angels into heaven also (2 Kgs. 2:11). He went up in one of their chariots of fire (cf. 2 Kgs. 6:18). The apostle John is taken to heaven and shown around the heavenly city by angels. Others in Scripture who are taken in spirit into heaven (to return to earth later) such as Daniel and Paul are also escorted by angels. There were angels present when Jesus ascended into heaven (Acts 1:9-11).

There is every reason to believe then that when we die our spirits will be escorted into heaven by angels. They accompany God's people everywhere, individually and collectively. In Jacob's dream (Gen. 28:12), we see the angels are perpetually traveling from heaven to earth and back again, ministering to the needs of God's people, following them wherever they go (Gen. 32:1). What a comforting thought to know not only will the angels carry us to heaven one day but they are watching over us here and now.

Children are assigned guardian angels who have instant access to God (Matt. 18:10). Peter apparently had a guardian angel (Acts 12), and Paul had angels taking care of him in prison and during his shipwreck (Acts 27:23). Phillip and Cornelius had angels direct them. Angels are assigned to each local church (Rev. 1-3), as well as to nations, Michael being the guardian angel of Israel. They are present at every worship service watching over our worship attitudes (Cor.11:10).

Throughout the Bible we see angels ministering to God's people on earth. They ministered to Christ while He was on earth. They were there strengthening Him at His temptation and again encouraging Him in the garden of Gethsemane. They were there at the resurrection and again at the ascension. Yes, guardian angels are for real (Psa. 91:11). They guard, guide, instruct, encourage and comfort all of God's people. They even appear to us sometimes without us realizing who they are (Heb. 13:2). Imagine the joy of meeting and getting to know your personal guardian angel one day in heaven!

1 Kings 22:20 shows the angels (heaven's host) having a board meeting discussion with God around His throne. Abraham had a dinner conversation with angels (Gen. 18). Lot had several heated discussions with them too (Gen. 19). Daniel, Peter, Paul and John also spoke with angels. The angels are obviously able to converse with men in any language they choose.

When on earth, whether disguised as men or seen as angels, these heavenly beings communicate freely, and intelligently with men. In heaven they communicate in the same way with God. In eternity we will be able to talk to angels just as freely as we talk to one another now. The passage in 1 Kings gives specific insight into their relationship with God. God asks for a volunteer to persuade Ahab to go into battle. He even agrees to one of the angel's suggestion that he go and confuse Ahab's prophets in order to accomplish this.

God is sovereign and already knew how to handle Ahab, but He loves for His servants to express their desire to carry out His will on earth. This applies to both angels and man. Even as God enjoys talking with the angels so we too will enjoy stimulating conversation with them one day in heaven.

Redemption is a mystery to the angels (1 Pet. 1:12). They cannot understand salvation by grace through faith at least not experientially. Because of our redemption in Christ, in heaven we will be higher than the angels. In fact we will judge them (1 Cor. 6:3). Though they are sent to minister to God's people they are also fellow servants with us (Rev. 22:9). As such they are to be respected for their spiritual power (cf 2 Pet. 2:10,11).

Because the angels were created separately they could not be redeemed through a representative head (ie. as in Adam so in Christ). Unlike man they do no procreate and are not descended from each other. They had to be judged on their individual obedience and loyalty to God.

Christ could not offer a substitutionary atonement for angels. He is not an angel. He could not stand in their place. Christ became a man to save man. Oh, I know He appeared in angel form prior to His incarnation as a man but He is not, nor ever was a created angel. He is the eternal God.

Only mankind was created in the total image of God. Only mankind was made to have true fellowship with Him and glorify His name forever. And God loved man above all His creation, so He sent His own Son to die for us (John 3:16). Because of Christ then, these amazing, beautiful, powerful creatures called angels are our ministers for all eternity, even as they are to God.

Will We Get to Meet the Angels of Scripture?

Michael, the Archangel, and Gabriel who spoke to Mary and all of the other angels of Scripture will serve the redeemed in heaven. What an awesome privilege to be ministered to by such personages. Yes, you will get to meet them all and call them by name. They may even become close friends.

Wouldn't you like to talk to the angels who appeared to the shepherds? Won't it be great to hear their side of that wonderful event? Or how about meeting the angels who administered the ten plagues of Egypt, or those who will pour out God's terrible judgments during the Tribulation? All the angels rejoice in heaven when a sinner gets saved. Imagine hearing how they all felt and reacted the day two of them rolled away Christ's tombstone?

As you read through the Scriptures note how often angels are part of the action. Then imagine meeting that particular angel one day in New Jerusalem and being able to hear their story. What wonderful conversations you are going to enjoy in heaven. What amazing relationships you will develop.

Hospitality towards strangers is encouraged in the church as well as showing love to those you know (Heb.13:1,2). Why? Because you may be entertaining an angel and not know it? Wow! Apparently angels still do visit earth in human form, yes even today. Few people ever see one though. Why? Because the Bible declares we won't recognize them!

I do believe from prophetic Scripture that angelic activity will increase on earth as the Lord's return draws near. We know during the Tribulation angels will be seen and heard on earth. They come to earth with a final declaration of the gospel as well as to announce judgment (Rev.14:6-7).

Of course, demonic activity will increase also as Satan knows the time left is short (Rev. 16:14). And this is the danger of believing every story of so-called angelic appearances today. In most instances they are either hoaxes, coincidences, or demonic activity. Remember Satan himself can appear as an angel of light.

Have I ever seen an angel? No! Have I been aware of their apparent presence? Yes, I believe so, on several occasions. Some one, other than myself, had control of the car during our terrifying crash that day. Call it coincidence if you like. I believe it was a guardian angel sent from God because it wasn't His time for us to die.

Perhaps many of you, like myself, have had the privilege of being at the bedside of a dying saint of God. As they passed peacefully into glory haven't you felt the presence of angels? Death is always ugly and cruel, yet for those who are at peace with the Lord there is a supernatural quality to their passing. It doesn't happen every time but when it does your neck hairs rise in apprehension yet your heart feels a glow of warmth all at he same time and you just know the Lord and His angels are right there in the room.

The Bible does say angels watch over the little children. Aren't you glad of that? It also declares the angels are present in church with us. They also watch over the affairs of government and nations. Even more amazing is the host of heaven all around you whenever you are engaged in God's work. Oh, that we had the faith of Elisha so we could actually see them. But they are there anyway. And they'll be there with us in eternity.

This parallel universe dimension of the spiritual realm of heaven is hard for us to grasp. I mean, no one, in their right mind, has ever really seen an angel or talked to one recently have they? So is heaven itself really real? What is reality anyway? Where is heaven now and can we be sure it is an actual place? If so, how can it help me today if I can't see it?

PART V.

A NEW DIMENSION

CHAPTER 18

IS HEAVEN FOR REAL?

What Is Reality?
Category 4 hurricanes can inflict immense property damage. Fortunately this particular system downgraded just before it came ashore. Nonetheless we heeded the warnings to evacuate. So did thousands of others, clogging the highways and filling every available motel room in the next four States. We spent the night huddled in the car, in the lee of a large church building. Two parents, two children, a cat and a dog, wondering if the car would get blown over by the buffeting winds and whether there would be anything left of our home the next day, if we ever made it back. It was a powerful reality check for the whole family.

"But Dad, what if our house is blown away? What about mom's car? What about all my things? It's just not fair!"

"Yea, Dad, what if the whole area is flooded? Where will we live? What will we do?"

Truly it was one of life's teachable moments!

"Kids, kids, listen up. If we have to start over, we can do that. Houses can be rebuilt. Things can be replaced. But let's thank God we still have each other. Our family is together, and we love each other. No storm can take that a way. All the things back home you think you just can't live without are only temporary

187

anyway. They'll wear out, you'll grow out of them or tired of them, and they'll get thrown out or given away. Only relationships last forever."

These are hard lessons to learn, even for adults. Only that which lasts forever is truly real, and worth living for. Everything else is insecure and temporary. No matter how real material things seem at the time, you can't take them with you. Someone else is going to have them after you if they don't deteriorate away. In this sense their accumulation and satisfaction is ultimately an illusion.

Only heaven lasts forever, its relationships *and* its material blessings. Heaven then by definition is the ultimate reality. What is reality? Heaven! What is truth? The One who came from heaven to bring us heaven.

Elisha was physically aware of the reality of heaven's presence when he confidently told his servant not to fear the Syrian army (2 Kgs. 6:16,17). Prayer enabled his servant to physically see the armies of heaven. Thus Heaven is a present reality, not just a future hope. In this aspect or dimension heaven is all around you.

Believers are already being blessed in heavenly places (Eph. 1:3). They sit together in heavenly places in Christ (Eph. 2:6). What does all this mean? It means a Christian can actually enter this fourth dimension, this parallel universe of heaven, in his spirit right now! Hebrews says our spirits enter the very throne room of God when we worship (Heb. 10:19-24). Wow! Let's think about this for a moment.

God and all the host of heaven are right there, all around you every day, wherever you are. They just happen to be in another dimension, on another plane as it were. Usually this dimension of heaven can only be accessed spiritually. However, God sometimes reveals this dimension of heaven physically, even today. Many accounts have been given of missionaries, and other believers in life-threatening situations, whom God has allowed to see the angel armies of heaven protecting them.

The Bible declares heaven is a present reality. This puts a whole new dimension (deliberate pun), on your prayer life and worship time. God himself, together with His angels, is present, in real time, whenever you engage in these activities. When I began to study this truth about the reality of heaven's presence it changed my whole attitude.

Now I pray and worship and read God's word with a new sense of excitement and reverence and awe. No longer can I rush into God's presence. No more can I sing worship songs without noticing and meaning the words. When I look to the front in church I see in my mind and spirit the very throne of God, hovering as it were above us. No, I haven't flipped my mind. Christ is there in the reality and glory of heaven. You just can't see Him visibly. You just can't access this new dimension physically yet.

Is Heaven the Final Answer?

Technology, however, is slowly destroying our sense of reality. What you see and hear and feel with your senses is no longer a reliable indicator of truth. Virtual reality systems make a mockery of what *is*. Truth can be so readily distorted by the high tech multi-media systems of today. So how can you make sense of it all? What is the final answer to life?

It is the intangibles of life that hold the key, the things that can't be measured by senses or science. Love, joy, peace, relationships, the eternal aspects of life are what it's all about. Heaven, remember, is the ultimate reality. It never changes. It goes on forever.

Heaven, then, is indeed the final answer to life. It is the final hope and purpose of life. Or rather He who offers you heaven, He who is the Life, is your final answer. What He freely offers you, by faith, is worth much more than a mere million-dollar jackpot. But perhaps there is no heaven or a God who really cares?

Creation all around you, or natural revelation as the theologians call it, tells you there is a God who designed and sustains everything. It also reminds you every day that there is an eternity to be hoped for. As Solomon puts it,

"God hath set the world in their heart, so that no man can find out the work that God maketh from the beginning to the end," (Eccl. 3:10).

189

The Hebrew word translated as *world* literally means *ceased* or *vanishing point* ie. eternity. When you look at the road ahead it visibly vanishes over the horizon in the distance. But you know it continues because it's going to take you to your destination beyond the horizon. So it is with life. God has set in your heart the instinctive knowledge that there is more, much more to this world, beyond the horizon of your brief life on this earth. Yet without God you are unable to figure out the end from the beginning or the purpose of life. Why has God put you here?

The Bible tells you it is to prepare you for eternity with Him. That's really what life is all about. Everything else is vanity, temporary and illusive. When it comes down to it, heaven really is the final answer to life. How can you be sure? Because God has said so in His word. He even became one of us, in time and recorded history, to make it possible for imperfect, fallen mankind to enter this perfect, holy, eternal place called heaven.

How Can I Be More Aware of Heaven Now?

Learn all you can about the heaven God has prepared for you. It will make you more aware of its present dimension.

"Set your affection on things above, not on things on the earth." (Col. 3:2).

Why? Because the things of earth are so temporary and illusive. Focus on the spiritual, first, and the rest of your life will fall into place. How can I do this? Pray, every day. Study God's word, every day. Trust Christ. And heaven will come to you.

"Seek those things which are above, where Christ sitteth on the right hand of God." (Col. 3:1).

Of course if you don't know Christ, what I've just said will appear as pious mumbo-jumbo Developing a spiritual life is the last thing most people want to think about. They refuse to acknowledge how close each of us are to eternity. No one knows what tomorrow will bring. But heaven gives you confidence God has already taken care of your tomorrows.

Hedonism, the Greek philosophy that life's purpose is pleasure and self-gratification, bombards you a thousand times a day. Countless billboards, TV and radio commercials, Hollywood movies, magazine and newspaper ads, scream at you to satisfy your feelings, now! If you can't touch it, taste it, hear it, see it, smell it, buy it, or email it, then it can't possibly give you any pleasure or satisfaction. It can't possibly exist! Therefore heaven is not real. Then neither is love or any other virtue or intangible of life?

Odd, isn't it? We can be motivated enough to spend money, by what we know is essentially a con-job, an advertisement. But we struggle to accept the word of our Creator and His free offer of salvation and heaven. But if heaven is so great, why can't I experience it now? You can!

Eternal life begins the moment you become a child of God. Here's where this new dimension, the spiritual realm of heaven comes into play. By faith (in Christ) your spirit is reborn so it can experience heaven now, even though your body and physical senses cannot (yet!). No, you can't enter the heavenly city, except through death or at the rapture. Yes, your spirit and even your heart and mind can become more and more aware of the spiritual realm of heaven all around you. You can, by faith, in prayer and worship, come before the very throne of God.

This is an awesome privilege, for the true believer in Christ. No, I am not talking about some mystical, out-of-body, meditation moment. I am speaking of having a relationship with the living God of heaven, of seeing Him work supernaturally in your life and the lives of fellow believers around you. Only the power of Christ from heaven can make you desire the spiritual more than the material. When He does, and begins to transform your life, you know heaven is real!

What Makes the Biblical Heaven So Special?

Resurrection is what makes the Biblical heaven the only one worth believing in. This is not some hoped for fantasy land made up by man's imagination of what he thinks he would like to do for all eternity. Nor is it some vague hope of endless recycling from one life form to another. Heaven is the truth, told by the only man that has ever died and come back to life, the only man who has come bodily from heaven, to assure us of it.

No other religious leader in history has ever claimed to be God in human form, or to have died and risen again and been seen by hundreds of eyewitnesses. If Jesus was a madman and these things were not historical fact, how come His enemies could not disprove them? How come His name has so influenced the world and history? How come thousands continue to give their lives for this man? Because He is who He claimed to be, the Son of God. Therefore what His word says about heaven is true and utterly reliable.

Jesus talked about heaven as a real, physical place He was preparing for His disciples (that includes you and me). He ascended back to this real place in a real physical body. The apostle John in the Book of Revelation gives us detailed descriptions of a very physical city that is part of this real place called heaven. The prophets of old wrote about this heavenly city also.

As we have examined throughout this book, the Bible gives us continuous types and patterns of this real place called heaven. The Biblical evidence for heaven as more than just some vague spiritual realm is overwhelming. There is no Scripture that says you will be sitting on a cloud playing a harp all day long! Yes, the elders and the angels are seen by John playing harps in the heavenly city (Rev. 5:8;14:2;15:2). Yes, there are clouds in heaven. Only Jesus is ever described as sitting on clouds and this is simply referring to His coming again in the clouds at the climax of the Tribulation judgments (Rev. 14:14).

How Does Heaven Help Me Face Death?

Fear of death and dying is overcome by the reality of heaven. Knowing there is a far more wonderful world awaiting the child of God after death helps you to face death with hope and a measure of serenity no matter what the circumstances. If heaven is the worst that can happen to you why should you be afraid of anything? Sure, there is healthy fear that tries to avoid disaster and unnecessary pain, but when self preservation is beyond your control you can fully trust the God of heaven to take care of you. Worry and panic won't help a bit.

Understanding the reality of heaven and the everlasting rest God has promised His children brings an almost inhuman (supernatural) ability to hope in the face of hopelessness. For the Christian never holds life cheaply, on the contrary, since his life now belongs to God and is being fitted for heaven, life becomes even more precious. Every extra moment God grants is an opportunity to glorify Him more, especially in the midst of pain and tragedy. Without hope of heaven there is only fear, anger, and despair.

Comfort and lasting solace for the aching heart at bereavement is only possible through the hope of heaven and the assurance of reunion. Without this hope the pain becomes unbearable. Only resurrection and the promise of eternal life makes any sense out of the loss of human life and the finality of death. For the believer, death is not the end but a glorious beginning, a commencement. The funeral becomes therefore a celebration for the one that has gone.

If you have ever attended the funeral of a true saint of God, you know what I am talking about. Though there is love and comfort and support for the family, the service itself is one of joy and hope and celebration rather than sadness and despair. Of course this would only be appropriate if heaven is real. And it is!

You see, only heaven, and its King, Jesus, can bring true comfort and hope in the face of death. He knows and understands. He wept at the effect death had on his friends, Mary and Martha, even though He knew He was about to raise their brother Lazarus to life again (John 11). He used this experience to teach the sisters about the reality of the resurrection and heaven.

How Does Heaven Help Me in the Day to Day?

Power, supernatural power to keep on going in the face of life's tragedies and trials, this is what the reality of heaven does for you in the day to day. Heaven reminds you your permanent home is

New Jerusalem, not where you live now. This perspective on life actually helps make you a better citizens. How so?

When you are not tied to material possessions, status or position, or the here and now, it frees you to work hard, give and even sacrifice to help make your town, city, country a better place for others. It doesn't even matter if you are never recognized for it. You will be in heaven.

As you begin to put into practice kingdom living now, in preparation for heaven, it should make you a model citizen. True followers of Christ care about the law, and justice, about their fellow man, and God's creation. They practice holiness and cleanliness and a good work ethic and they treat others with respect. Through the spirit of Christ within them they bring a little heaven to earth.

"Thy will be done on earth as it is in heaven."

Rewards for what you are becoming; loving, kind, peaceful, patient, rather than for what you accomplish and accumulate, makes heaven a special place. It changes your priorities. Focusing on relationships and spiritual development become more important in the light and hope of heaven. Heaven and eternity remind you too, of the brevity of life and the need to use your time wisely.

When you realize the reality of heaven, the God of heaven becomes the most important person in your life. His will and His glory is the only thing that really matters. This brings a tremendous freedom to living. If you have done what pleases God, it doesn't matter what others say. It doesn't matter if you have not finished all the other priorities of your day. Tomorrow will take care of itself.

"Seek first the kingdom of heaven . . ."

Like Jesus said, worrying won't add anything to your life. So quit sweating the small stuff and rest in Him.

When you finally understand that your eternal destiny is more important (and far more lasting) than your immediate goals in life, it helps you set the right priorities. Heaven really has a way of clarifying our lives for us. That's why it's so important you know what the Bible teaches about heaven. It is a real, live, tangible place to hope for. Yet not everyone gets to go there!

Does Heaven Really Make Sense?

Ecclesiastes tells us everyone knows there is an eternity to hope for, that this life is not all there is. Our hearts and consciences know there is a God in heaven to whom we must give account. We know there is a heaven to gain and a hell to avoid, else this short and troubled life is pointless. Man is spiritual and different from the animals. We are without excuse when we refuse to respond to the evidence all around us (Rom. 1:18-22). Only the fool has said in his heart there is no God (Psa. 14:1).

What is the point in doing good or being good if there is no heaven? Why not just live for pleasure and survival? Yet if we sink to the level of the animals, dominate or be dominated, life becomes meaningless. Yes, but this ensures the strongest and fittest survive, the evolutionist will say. History shows us the opposite. We self destruct when everyone lives by this ethic. Empires have destroyed themselves because of such pride and selfishness. No, we are made in the image of God, for His pleasure and glory. And He is Holy!

Also, if God is Creator and a personal being, then He must live and reign somewhere in time and space. And He does, in a perfect, holy place called heaven. If, as the Bible declares, He longs to live forever with His special creation, mankind, then He surely has prepared a special place for us in His heaven. Heaven does make sense. It is the ultimate reality.

But if I can't see heaven, it's still only a concept isn't it, not a real place? So was North America . . . until Columbus! Remember, back then they thought he would fall off the edge of the world trying to get there! And even Columbus didn't know America existed. He thought it was India. But when he came back alive to tell the tale, the whole world believed and wanted to go there.

Jesus came from heaven to tell you all about it. Just because you can't see it, or photograph it, or record, or measure heaven, does not mean it isn't there. Like electricity or gravity you see its influence and by faith, therefore, you believe it. Besides, you have the written record of Old Testament prophets and the apostle John and countless other individuals, people like yourself, who have seen into heaven and told you what it is like.

These eyewitness accounts are more reliable, accurate, incredibly uniform and trustworthy than almost any other historical record ever written. We don't doubt what is written about the great leaders and philosophers of the Roman empire, or the people of Greece, Egypt, Persia and ancient China. Yet much of this written record is biased, sketchy, contradictory, and written years after the events. The Biblical history, though questioned often, has never been disproved yet. In fact the more archeology discovers, the more it confirms the incredible accuracy of the Biblical record.

What I am saying is that we have a reliable written record of heaven by people who have seen it first hand. Most of all we have the record of Jesus' own teaching on heaven. He is the King of heaven and is there right now. One day He is coming back to earth to take His followers there.

So what is the essence of this place called heaven? What are the special relationships of heaven? Why are relationships so important there? What will my relationships be like? Will I make new friends there? Who will be my special friends?

CHAPTER 19

IT'S ALL ABOUT PEOPLE

What Is the Essence of Heaven?

Crowds of people jostled together in the dining room line-up. Happy voices and intermittent laughter filled the packed hall. I scanned the sea of faces hoping to find a familiar one. It had been a lonely flight all the way from the East coast to this California conference. It would be a lonely week if I didn't find someone I knew here.

"Hey, Larry, want to break out of this crush and find a decent place to eat?"

I turned to see who had addressed me and there was a dear friend and colleague whom I hadn't seen for years. We never wrote, rarely called, and only occasionally met together at national conferences. Yet it was as if we had never moved away. Our relationship, our conversation, our concern for each other was just the same as when he beat up on me at racquetball every week and we shared together the struggles, frustrations and joys of our early days of ministry.

Relationships! It's really what life is all about. It's also what heaven is all about. Here on earth the worst experiences and the humblest places are often remembered with joy because of the love and acceptance of relationships there. Conversely, the best of experiences and the most magnificent of places are sometimes totally marred because of devastating relationships. The city of

God will be an incredible place to live not so much for its beauty and awesomeness but for the relationships, first with God and then with everyone else.

Joyful times of fellowship await us in heaven. Every relationship will begin with child-like, absolute trust. They will progress from there towards spiritual intimacy, a oneness of heart, mind and spirit that will satisfy the deepest longing of your soul. You will have all eternity to develop relationships with the millions of saints there. It will take you forever to become as close to your fellow believers as the relationship is between the Father, Son and Holy Spirit.

No matter what you do, physically or spiritually in heaven, it will be enhanced by beautiful personal relationships, beginning with Christ and extending to the millions of new people you will meet with, work with, worship with and get to know. A study of the Biblical words that relate to eternity and forever, and the everlasting intangibles of the character of God and His dwelling place, heaven, paint a wonderful picture of *people*, and all the things people do together.

God is a personal God who created personal beings in His image so He could enjoy relating to them forever. As we have said again and again, the real joy and excitement of heaven is being with God and with His people, much more than the material rewards and opulent splendor there. Heaven is where the family of God lives. The heavenly city is our home-town.

It is this word *home* that best describes the essence of heaven. Even living in a ramshackle home here on earth can be special to us because of the people we share it with. They matter to us much more than the décor. Imagine living in a magnificent mansion in a perfect new world, where everyone is family? This is what heaven is all about . . . people . . . warm, loving, beautiful people .

Eternity is for building relationships. Eternal life itself is the ongoing act of knowing God. Worship in the heavenly city will be a large part of knowing God, as you come before His throne each day. Celebrating, eating and rejoicing, and thanking God together will be a large part of knowing others. If you don't like people you won't enjoy heaven. But then we'll all be perfect there!

Will I Make New Friends in Heaven?

Yes, you will make millions of new friends in heaven. It will be so easy to do, considering everyone we meet will be kind and loving and trusting. There will always be time for this, all the time in the world. Life will just get better and better as your circle of intimate friends grows ever larger.

But won't I eventually know everyone? Perhaps you will finally get to meet everyone at least once, but it will take forever to become intimate friends with them all. Remember part of knowing God is to become ever more like Him and He knows each one of us absolutely and loves everyone of us totally and unconditionally.

Serving together in Christ's kingdom will give us endless opportunities to meet new people and really get to know them. Learning new tasks and skills as we serve Christ together will open up further opportunities to develop and deepen relationships. Dining together at the endless feasts and celebrations of heaven will be another avenue of relationship development. Just as you have tasted here on earth!

For many people some of their closest friends are their work buddies. This is especially true if you have ever worked together in a volunteer, service environment. Serving in the local church, traveling together on Mission work projects, volunteering at local charities, or simply helping out a neighbor can develop a very special closeness. It will be like this all the time in heaven.

Or how about those friendships you made in school or college? Sweating out exam time with your study mates often makes for great friendships. Imagine learning from the Master and the masters, some new skill in heaven.

What great friends your fellow learners will become. Or perhaps you will be one of the masters teaching others and developing new friends with your students. In all of these examples you will inevitably, at some point, celebrate and dine together, just like Christ promised He would do with the disciples (Matt. 26:29). Yes, you will still enjoy meals together in heaven. In fact their main benefit will be growing relationships rather than growing waistbands! What a wonderful social life we have awaiting us in heaven.

What About Family Relationships?

Brother and sister relationships on earth can be some of the closest we experience. When you are brought up together, living in the same house, sharing possessions, responsibilities, successes, disappointments and the same parental authority, it creates a very special bond. Twins enjoy an even closer unity. Jesus said that anyone who does the will of God the Father is His brother or sister. In heaven everyone, at least within our initial family unit, will seem like a twin brother or sister. Over time (eternity) we will grow to love the whole populous of heaven in the same way.

This makes renewing and deepening sibling and other family relationships here and now of prime importance to God and to your own preparation for heaven. If you haven't spent time working on your relationships here on earth, you won't somehow be magically and instantly close in heaven. Even in eternity, relationships will take time to grow. Remember, relationships are the only thing you can take with you into eternity, so make time for them now. It will make your initial entrance into heaven so much more exciting and rewarding.

Make friends on earth, share the gospel with your family, so they can be with you forever in heaven. Yes, you'll be part of a special family unit in heaven. But building the relationships of your heavenly family began the moment, by faith, you received eternal life. Heavenly relationships start now, at home and in church!

Family members you are especially close to now will continue to be so in heaven. Spiritual colleagues you have served with in ministering to others will continue to be part of your close circle of friends in heaven. Those you have discipled and those who discipled you will have a special relationship with you in eternity. Jesus enjoyed a special relationship with a close circle of friends on earth, His disciples. We know they enjoy a special place in the heavenly city. We know therefore they continue to enjoy a special relationship to Jesus and with one another in eternity.

We will enjoy special relationships in heaven, first with our earthly spouses and those related to us, then all these relationships we have just talked about. Not that anyone will ever feel left out or snubbed or lonely in heaven. Relationships will not be exclusive, just special. Oh, that we would spend more time on them now! Human relationships are important. They are a vital part of eternity. But the most important relationship of all is our relationship to Christ.

Worship in heaven is centered on the person of Jesus Christ. Without a personal relationship to Him, worship is meaningless and boring and so is the thought of serving Him forever. Those who don't know Him won't be there anyway. For the redeemed, this is what we have been waiting for, to see Christ and know Him forever.

What an incredible moment to finally meet Jesus face to face and hear Him say "Well done." In glory He will be our Lord, the King upon the throne in New Jerusalem, and we will honor Him as such. Yet He will also be our brother and friend who will work with us, and walk and talk with us often. What fascinating contrasts this relationship will offer. On the one hand you will have spiritual intimacy with the God of the Universe and on the other you will enjoy the physical presence and friendship of the Son, while all the time acknowledging and beholding His glory.

He already knows everything about you. In heaven you begin to learn more and more about Him as you share daily in His glory. This relationship will never end, it will only get better and better. Adam enjoyed a taste of this, before the Fall. This is what mankind was made for. Adam walked with God after working in the garden God had specially prepared for Him. You will walk with Christ in heaven after working in His kingdom on the new earth. So what will your working relationships be like?

Nations on the new earth will require leaders and workers, in order to operate in harmony with the rest of Christ's kingdom. Just as today, there will be leaders and staff to carry out kingdom projects and the day-to-day running of countries. But, remember Christ said His work is easy and His burden light. Work will be nothing like the rat-race of today. It will seem more like a family project, which in essence it is. This will be true whether the work is on a national level or on a local level within the cities of the new earth.

Just as on the earth today, so in heaven, work will enable you to meet and make new friends and relationships. Once again heaven is about people. Heaven is first about relationships, not work. Work in heaven is simply part of the privilege of reigning with Christ. It is an expression of our relationship to Him. Serving Christ, throughout all eternity is one of the joyful privileges of heaven. Worshipping Him daily in the throne-room of New Jerusalem will be the highlight of your days there. Deepening a close, personal relationship with the Lord of the universe will be the real bliss of eternity.

To the unbeliever these statements may seem to be contradictory and not things to be looked forward to. To those who have already surrendered their lives to Him, and have seen and understood what they have been saved from, they are the epitome of heaven. The greatest glory, joy, and wonder of eternity will be the privilege of knowing and living with Christ, in intimate relationship, forever and ever.

Will I Ever Be Alone in Heaven?

Instant translation from one place to another in heaven means, in one sense, you need never be alone. On the other hand it also allows for you to instantly get away from it all, to the farthest reaches of the universe if necessary. Though inner city life is rarely quiet, even New Jerusalem has peaceful gardens and wide open spaces to be alone in. Christ's kingdom is one of peace, a peace that will never end.

All this emphasis on relationships may make you think you can never be alone in heaven. That's just not true. Jesus frequently took time alone, away even from His disciples. He would head for the hills or the lake shore. You will still be able to do the same in heaven. "In quietness and confidence shall be your strength" God says (Isa.30:15). Isaiah prophecies God's people will one day live in peaceful homes in quiet resting places (Isa. 32:18). He even explains the work of righteousness is peace and quietness (Isa. 32:17).

So, yes, you will be able to get away from the crowd, to be still and know that He is God. The new earth will have wonderful places to visit away from the cities and the people. Quietness is part of holiness (1 Pet. 3:4). Quietness will be part of our relationships in heaven, in the sense of there never being any strife or anger or tension in them. Once again there are beautiful contrasts in heaven, from joyful feasting and exciting relationships to quiet, peaceful times alone, enjoying the splendor of the new earth or perhaps exploring the vast stillness of outer space.

Adam, we have noted, had a tremendous relationship with the animal kingdom. Baalam even spoke to an animal. So what will our relationship be to creation and God's creatures? Similar to the beginning, we will again share in Christ's dominion and control over His creation. The universe will be unaffected by sin so we can develop unique understanding and even special relationships with all of God's creatures in heaven. They will simply become another enhancement to our personal relationships with one another.

Our love of domestic pets today is but a taste of what it will be like with all the creatures of heaven. Isaiah's beautiful picture of the millennial kingdom points also to eternity, where the wolf and the lamb, the leopard and the kid, the lion and the calf, the cow and the bear and even the snake all live quietly together (Isa. 11:4-9). What a wonderful world Christ has in store for you! But back to the human relationships, will I get to know the great heroes of the past? Of course!

Patriarchs and other Biblical heroes are specifically mentioned in the Bible's hall of fame of faith (Heb.11). They will all be there in heaven. You will indeed have the opportunity to develop relationships with them. Jesus promised His disciples this. Perhaps some of them will even turn out to be your family ancestors, or perhaps your spiritual forefathers. And this applies to all the great heroes of earth's history that make it into heaven.

Even if you don't have immediate, close family ties with these men and women, there will be ample opportunity to begin a relationships with them as you live and work and worship together in Christ's kingdom. What an awesome prospect to spend a day with Moses or David or Daniel or John or Wesley or Moody or Spurgeon! The list could be endless. The day could become weeks. There won't be enough time, too many people will want to do the same! But this is eternity! There will always be enough time. There will be endless opportunities to meet new people and build relationships. But who am I to spend time with such heroes of faith? Won't there be some kind of spiritual class distinction in heaven?

Rewards in heaven, as we have noted, will not be evenly distributed. Some will always have more than others. Responsibilities will vary too. Some will always have special authority over others in heaven. But everyone will be accepted, not for their position, authority or possessions, but for who they are in Christ. In Him we are all equal. Like husband and wife we are "Heirs together of the grace of life" (1 Pet. 3:7).

So, yes, there will be different roles and responsibilities in heaven but never any kind of social class distinctions. Everyone will treat everyone else with the same love and respect. After all, the heroes of faith and history only became such because of God's sovereignty in their lives. Plus they had the help and influence of many, many people, beginning with their parents. In heaven you will see and understand all this. From God's perspective, he who plants and he who waters are equally important but it is God alone who brings the growth (1 Cor. 3:6-8).

This is so foreign to our worldly way of thinking, of course. We find it hard to separate money, power, position and influence from success and respect, regardless of character. We assume it was all attained through personal will and effort and even chance, not God's mercy and grace and the help of others.

On earth we often see those with the greatest character having little status and few possessions, just like Jesus. If you act with honesty, integrity and humility you'll inevitably get overlooked for promotion and taken advantage of by others. And you'll certainly never make it onto any TV Talk Shows! In heaven it will not be that way. The humblest will receive the greatest honor.

Not that there won't be rich and successful people with great responsibility in heaven. Abraham and David were hardly without money and influence on earth. It's just that in heaven we will consider the rich and famous as equals, and they will of us. Their authority in the kingdom will not prevent you becoming close friends. You'll never feel inferior there.

Why Are Relationships So Important?

Fellowship with God is the reason we are created. Relationships with others made in His image is an expression of fellowship with Him. God saw it was not good for Adam to be alone, even though he walked with God every day. So He made Eve, instituted the family and commanded Adam and Eve to procreate and fill the earth. Family relationships became a secondary reason for our existence.

Everywhere you look in the Bible, relationships are paramount. This is what all the stories are about. God's relationship to us and our relationships with one another. They are the key to life, eternal life, knowing God. In America we pride ourselves on our independence. We honor those who are self-made successes. Yet there is really no such individual. Somewhere along the line he had to rely on relationships for his success. Man cannot survive alone. Babies die if they are not touched and talked to. We know all this and yet we spend so little time developing close relationships with God or others, compared to the time we spend on physical, temporal and material things.

Relationships can be eternal. Heaven is eternal. Heaven is all about relationships. When God lives in intimate fellowship with His people, this is heaven. When the people of God live in perfect fellowship with one another, this is heaven. So where do these heavenly relationships develop?

Home is where the heart is. God desires to make our hearts His home. When the Holy Spirit takes up residence within your heart, through faith in Christ, this is when and where heaven begins. Without this personal relationship to God, there is no entrance into heaven. Without His Spirit within you, you can never develop perfect fellowship with others.

Thus heaven begins on earth, the spiritual kingdom of God in the hearts of all His people. You can begin to develop heavenly relationships with Christ and His followers, now, through His church, the visible body of Christ on earth. You develop your relationship to God when you come before His throne in worship and prayer and Bible study. So too in heaven you will develop your relationship with Him in the throne room of New Jerusalem. We develop relationships with our spiritual family on earth as we worship, serve and work together for the kingdom. So too in the final kingdom of heaven, the new earth and new universe.

Entrance into heaven depends on a restored relationship to God. Sin has broken this relationship. Only through faith in Christ's sacrificial payment for our sin, confirmed by His resurrection, can a holy, perfect God accept sinners again into fellowship with Him. This is why having a personal relationship to God, through Christ is so important. Without it you will never see the wonderful place this book has been talking about. We will talk more about this in the final chapter.

Perhaps you can see the implications of all this talk about relationships. Relationships should become a priority in our lives. First, we must make time to develop our relationship to God through Christ. We need to work more on the spiritual aspect of our lives, not only to prepare for heaven but to get the most out of life now! Jesus came to give us abundant life now, not just in eternity. Then we need to give more time and attention to our human relationships than perhaps we do now. Life is short. Time lost can't be redeemed.

In the end, isn't it human relationships that give us the most satisfaction out of life? Isn't having a clear conscience and being at peace with God even more satisfying? "For what shall it profit a man, if he gain the whole world, and lose his own soul?" (Mark 8:36).

So are you ready for heaven? Are you sure you're going there? What about hell? Is there really such a place? Is heaven really worth living for?

CHAPTER 20

ARE YOU READY FOR FOREVER?

Why Worry about Heaven Now?

"Dad, dad, come look at the television. A plane just flew into a building in New York City. They said it was a jumbo jet."

"Yea, right. I doubt that. It was probably just some guy in a Cessna that got lost."

"No! no! You can see the smoke and flames pouring out. Come and look."

I was sure my college-aged daughter was exaggerating and I told her to quit watching TV and get off to class. Nevertheless I hurried into the living-room and watched in shocked fascination what seemed like a "towering inferno" movie scene. Moments later another jetliner crashed into the adjacent twin tower of the New York Trade Center in a burst of flame. Yet it all seemed so surreal. Was this just a Hollywood movie or real life?

By the time Rebecca and I watched the Trade Towers crumble to the ground in that fearful cloud of dust, and heard the reports of a terrorist attack, the reality of it all sank in. Every time they replayed the plane impacts, and the towers collapsing, I couldn't get out of my mind I was watching thousands of unsuspecting people pass instantly into eternity.

I am sure when they set out for work that morning few of these individuals ever dreamed they would be facing their Maker before lunch! What a sobering thought. None of us knows what tomorrow will bring, terrorists or no terrorists. Each day is a gift from God.

Are you ready for forever? Where will you spend eternity? Well, maybe it all just ends at death? You know in your heart that's not true. Your own conscience and all creation around you tells you there is a God, there is a hereafter. You instinctively know there has to be order and purpose to life despite the evil all around you. But why does a loving God allow such evil to exist? Why doesn't He do something about the terrorists of our world?

Why Does God Allow evil?

God is never the author of evil, man is. Disasters happen because we live in a fallen world. Yes, God is sovereign and controls everything, but not the human will. We still have freedom of moral choice. So how is He in control then? By His grace He is able to bring eternal good even out of man's evil acts. The cross and resurrection are the ultimate demonstration of this principle.

Also, in His mercy He prevents things being even worse. Usually we don't understand this. We are too selfishly complaining about was has happened to stop and consider how much worse it could have been. We forget to thank God for the countless times He has protected us from other disasters. It is amazing how fear goes away when you count your blessings instead of cursing the darkness.

But how can any good come out of the Trade Center attacks? Why did those innocent people have to die? Were they being judged of God? Of course not. Evil happens in a sin-sick world . . . to the good and the bad. Jesus answered similar kinds of questions about Pilate's unfair massacre of worshipers in the temple, and about the Tower collapse in Siloam, which killed several innocent people. (Luke 13:1-5). His listeners assumed those killed somehow deserved it because the events were so tragic and unexpected.

"I tell you," He said, "Except ye repent ye shall all likewise perish."

What was He saying here? Was He being unkind? No, He was saying every disaster should remind us of our own mortality, and the need to be in a right standing with God. I am sure millions of people reconsidered their eternal destiny after the September 11 attacks. Indeed all of America momentarily turned to God for understanding, comfort and protection, led by a President who wisely called us to prayer. It unified a nation, restored national pride, and prompted an outpouring of sacrificial giving, of money, time and effort.

By the way, God will take care of the terrorists, even if we don't. Read Psalm 37 to see how He deals with the wicked, now as well as in eternity. Even David though, found it almost too painful to bear when he saw evil men go unpunished, and even prospering from their crimes. That is until he went into God's house and prayed. Then he understood their final end (Psalm 73:16,17).

But why do we have to consider our eternal destiny? If God is a loving God why doesn't everyone go to heaven? God is just and holy. He cannot ignore sin, and evil, and remain true to His own nature. Do you really believe Osama bin Laden should not be brought to justice for the horrors he orchestrated? If our sense of justice is riled by acts of terrorism how much more is the holiness of a perfect God violated by the sins of all mankind.

This may be hard to accept but God would still be just if he condemned the whole human race to hell. He has to judge sin and the sinner. None of us are perfect (as God is). But yes, God is love too, and has found a way to forgive the sinner without violating his own justice and holiness.

But salvation is a gift and God will not control your free will. You must choose for yourself whether you want to spend eternity with God or without Him.

But why would anyone not want to go to heaven? Because many just refuse to admit they are sinners who need saving. Yet without repentance (conviction of sin) and belief in (not just about) God's Son there is no remission of sin or entrance to heaven. It's that simple and that hard. It is sheer pride that makes us believe we are in control of our own destiny and to say there is no God.

So What Is the Alternative to Heaven?

Separation from God forever is the only alternative to heaven. Essentially this is the definition of hell. Well, that doesn't sound so bad. Except for one thing. Every human being has been given an eternal spirit created to have fellowship with God. Apart from Him we are unfulfilled, empty and lost. Many never acknowledge this on earth but at the Judgment it will become inescapable.

If you can imagine a child being torn from its mother to be sold into slavery you have a tiny glimpse of the agony of a human soul torn from his Creator and sent to hell. Why am I talking about hell in a book on heaven? If there's a heaven to be gained there must be a hell to avoid. Mere logic, as well as God's Word, demands this.

Besides which, the One who came from heaven, Jesus, talked more about hell than anyone else in Scripture. Why would He do this? Out of love for a lost mankind. Even an earthly father will warn his children of dangers they don't yet see or understand.

Luke 16 teaches hell is a place of torment and deep regret (Luke 16:19-31). Hell and the final lake of fire were created for Satan and his followers, the fallen angels (Matt.25:14). Those who reject Christ are sent to join them (Rev. 20:14,15). Jesus frequently used the word *gehenna* for hell in describing its everlasting fires and torments (Mark 9: 45,46).

Gehenna, which means "valley of Hinnom" was a garbage dump ravine outside of Jerusalem which was perpetually burning. In its previous history it had been the place where the Canaanites gave their children in bloody sacrifice to Moloch and where the bones of the dead were thrown. In the eyes of the Jews it had become a place of fear, horror, death and burning. It was definitely a place to avoid! In using this term to describe hell Jesus makes it very clear to His Jewish listeners just what the eternal destiny of the wicked is like. Obviously hell is not literally in a valley outside of Jerusalem, so where is it located?

Beneath the earth (the pit), beneath the sea (the abyss, the deep), this is where hades, sheol, the place of the dead and hell are found (Psa. 71:20; Prov. 15:24; Isa. 14:9). Hell is constantly referred to as being *beneath* heaven and the earth. Apparently this is both its spiritual and physical location. It is entirely separated from God and His throne, it is the ultimate place of separation from Him.

Hell is a place of outer and utter darkness beyond the light of day or the light of God (1 Sam. 2:9; Matt. 18:12). It will be lit only by the everlasting flames of torment which the wicked may only feel, not see, blindly groping through the darkness forever. Jesus taught those in hell will be fully conscious, in mind, body and spirit, and it will last forever. But how could a loving God send anyone to such a horrible place, and then condemn them there forever? He doesn't!

Why Would God Send Anyone to Hell?

Independence, pride, selfishness, cause men to reject God. They want the freedom to choose their own morality (just like Adam and Eve!), and to be accountable to no one, least of all a God they can't even see. Separated from God (by choice) they suffer the inevitable consequence of their unrepentent lifestyles, in this world and the next. Read the list of people who will never inherit the kingdom of God (1 Cor. 6:9-10; Gal. 5:19-21). Just remember, when you read this list, God is a holy God, not a politically correct one!

Sin, by definition, is anything less than perfection, which condemns us all! So ultimately it is not just sinful acts that send people to hell (we all sin). It is the willful decision to reject Christ, God's only remedy for sin. Jesus died to forgive us our sin and make us holy, not just to offer us heaven.

Men (and women) freely choose therefore, to go to hell, God does not arbitrarily send them. They choose not to submit to the Lordship of Christ. They don't want Him to transform them into holy people fit for heaven. Don't blame God. Blame the sinner. So how can I be sure I'm going to heaven? I'm glad you asked.

Faith, you remember, is something we can't get through life without. The issue is, who do we put our faith in.

"He that believeth (has faith in, trusts his life to) on the Son hath everlasting life: and he that believeth not the Son shall not see life (Jn. 3:36).

211

This is the promise of God's Word:

"For whosoever shall call upon the name of the Lord shall be saved" (Rom. 10:13). "If thou shalt confess with thy mouth the Lord Jesus and shalt believe in thine heart that God hath raised him from the dead thou shalt be saved" (Rom. 10;9).

Are you saying then, only Christians go to heaven? Isn't that a bit arrogant, narrow minded, and intolerant of you? No, because I didn't say it. God did!

"Jesus saith unto him, I am the way, the truth, and the life: no man cometh unto the Father but by me" (John 14:6).

So, all the other world religions are wrong and God doesn't care about the Muslim, Hindu or Buddhist? Well, first, no *religion* is able to save anyone, no matter how sincere or devout they are. Only a *relationship* to God ensures entrance into heaven. God has said His Son, Jesus Christ, is the only One who can restore that relationship.

"Neither is there salvation in any other: for there is none other name under heaven given among men, whereby we must be saved." (Acts 4:12).

Second, God loves the Muslim, Hindu, Buddhist and everyone else in this world (even the atheist), enough to send His Son to die for them so they might all have access to heaven, through faith in Christ. God is pleased with those of any religion who truly seek Him, and who strive to live godly lives. Read the story of the Roman soldier in Acts 10. God also promises those who seek Him with all their heart will find Him (Jer. 29:13). But, just as in Acts 10, He will always, somehow, bring the true message of the gospel of Jesus Christ to those who seek Him. This is the only way to heaven.

Truth is truth. There can't be any alternatives. If penicillin is the only cure for your child's sickness, the only medication that will save his life, you're not going to ask the doctor to prescribe an alternative just because other drugs have healing properties, your grandmother always used them, or they happen to be cheaper? They may make him feel better but he'll still die. God says faith in Christ's death and resurrection is the *only* cure for the sickness of man's sin.

I know, I know, you've probably heard all this before. Just remember though, you are saved *by faith*, not anything you do (Eph. 2:8,9). Salvation is a gift. So accept it, by faith, and you can be sure you're on your way to heaven.

"These things have I written unto you that believe in the name of the Son of God, that ye may *know* that ye have eternal life ((1 Jn. 5:13).

So once I am in heaven will I still be aware of those in hell?

God promises there will be no more crying, sorrow, death or pain in heaven (Rev. 21:4). In His presence is fullness of joy (Psa. 16:11). Given that the Bible will be in heaven, obviously you will still know of hell's existence. However, like the memories of the old earth, the glories of heaven will overwhelm any negative thoughts of the past. You won't be able to communicate with those in hell nor will you even think about them anymore.

We are promised peace in heaven. How could anyone be at peace and think about hell, let alone be physically made aware of it? Remember hell is total separation from the presence of God. Heaven is the continuous, glorious presence of God and this is where we will be. No, you will not be aware of hell in heaven.

How Do I Prepare for Heaven?

Worship with other believers in God's house on His day prepares you for heaven's throne room. Reading, studying, learning, applying God's word, the Bible, prepares you to know God and therefore experience eternal life, now. Sharing your faith in Christ with others, reaching out in love to the hurting, serving humbly and willingly in your church, prepares you for living in that heavenly city one day.

So how does living as a Christian in the world prepare you for heavenly relationships? It teaches you to love unconditionally, and unselfishly. Such Christ-like attitudes and witness inevitably will bear fruit in the lives of others, others who may now join you one day in heaven.

The church is God's major instrument to prepare you for heaven. It is His body and His bride on earth and the only way you can mature as a believer and learn what heavenly living is all about. Imperfect as it is, it is the family of God on earth. By the way, if you ever find a perfect church it won't be as soon as you join it! Just kidding, but you know what I mean.

Check out the seven churches in the first three chapters of Revelation. None of them were perfect, yet each one is used of God to prepare believers for heaven, or at least a remnant within them. A good Bible-believing, loving, witnessing church is the best place in the world to prepare for heaven. But don't focus on the people in the church, they will often let you down. Look to the Lord of the church and His word and you'll keep growing in Him.

Relationships with other believers in the local church make it possible to experience heaven on earth now. These relationships are just so different from the ones you generally experience during the working week. Christians really care. True worship with believers of like mind, no matter what your form of worship may be, can also be a taste of heaven now. The joy of knowing you are part of a wider family than your own, even across the world, as well as in your own church, brings heaven a little closer.

Heaven is all around you if you look for it. Every cup of cold water given in Christ's name, every word of encouragement or touch of love is a taste of heaven. Share a little heaven with someone else. It will build rewards and relationships for you in heaven one day. Heaven really is worth living for.

Peace in your heart, peace in your home, peace in your work, peace about your future, peace with God, this is what Christ and His heaven brings. This is why heaven is worth living for. Unfortunately, for most today, they know no such peace. Power for living above the chaos all around, power to be at peace even when life's disasters come, this is what living for heaven is all about. Assurance of heaven and eternity brings deep peace and purpose to life.

Heaven is real. It is a tangible, physical place already prepared for God's people. We will live in a world very similar to this earth, only even more glorious. I am convinced of this because of the great, recurring themes throughout the Bible. If you have ever disciplined yourself to read through the Bible, from Genesis to Revelation, in two or three sittings, just as you would read a novel, you will understand what I am about to explain.

When you read through the whole Bible in this way you begin to see the tremendous flow of God's revelation, even though many of the books and events are not in strict chronological order. More than this, it highlights the repeated themes, types and patterns of Scripture in a way which studying these things in their individual passages doesn't accomplish. You begin to see there is indeed nothing new under the sun (Eccl. 1:9). God made everything perfect the first time and He doesn't change His perfect way of doing things. It was man who messed up.

When God makes everything new (*kainos* /renew) again (Rev. 21:5), He will do so in a very similar way. Heaven, the new earth and universe, will be much like the present universe, minus the effects of sin. Given the added spiritual dimension, it will of course be even more glorious and wonderful than before. I hope the insights gleaned from all this and shared here will help make heaven a much more real place to you.

What's the Most Exciting Thing about Heaven?

Living with God is the most exciting thing about heaven. If you don't know Him personally yet this won't make sense to you. Relationships, with Christ, with other believers, and with the angels, this will definitely be a huge part of the excitement of heaven. The incredible love experienced in heavenly relationships makes it the most exciting place you've ever dreamed about.

We all like to be liked. Deep down we all long to love and be loved. It is part of the image of God in us. This is why John 3:16 is the most memorized verse in the Bible, because it tells us we are loved. It tells us Christ loved us enough to die for us.

Heaven is filled with this kind of agape (unselfish, Christ-like) love. Wow! What an environment to live in, forever and ever. It gives you a warm glow just to think about it!

Seeing, and knowing and loving and being loved by the very God of the universe, our Savior, Lord and Creator, is an awesome prospect to look forward to. Think, remember, the most spiritual moment you have ever experienced so far, when you felt so close to God you could almost touch Him, and your heart burned within you. Remember the excitement, the joy, the peace, the power of that spiritual high. It was but a taste of heaven. The best is yet to come.

New Jerusalem, that dazzling city in the sky, is surely the next most exciting thing about heaven. Or how about our incredible new bodies, forever young and vibrant, bursting with life and supernatural power? Then there's the beautiful new earth with its pristine environment, awesome vistas, spotless cities and tame animals.

We could go on and on about the stars and space and vast new galaxies, the nations and cultures, the mansions, the wealth, the family gatherings, the banquets, the music, and the worship services. How good the Lord is, to share all this inheritance with us forever and ever. What a wonderful, exciting future is in store for all those who come to God through Christ. How good to know there is a glorious hereafter. This life on earth does have a point and purpose to it. There is hope. There is peace. There is a God. There is a heaven.

Promises in the Bible, of all the things we have looked at concerning heaven, assure us we will be happy there. The pleasures of heaven continue forever, the psalmist tells us. We will come into the presence of God's glory with exceeding joy, Jude writes (Jude 24).

"I go to prepare a (real) place for you" Jesus assured His disciples.

Perhaps before, when you heard about worshipping with angels before the throne, or serving the Lord, or walking on gold streets, or simply the endlessness of forever, you wondered if you would like heaven. Will I really be happy there? I hope this book has alleviated some of those thoughts for you. I trust it has made you more aware of the reality of the hope which is laid up for you in heaven (Col. 1:5).[3]

Of course, the Biblical picture of heaven I have tried humbly to present to you here is but a glimpse of what it will be like.

"Eye hath not seen, nor ear heard, neither have entered into the heart of man, the things which God hath prepared for them that love him. But God hath revealed them unto us by his Spirit" (1 Cor. 2:9,10).

Too often the last part of this verse is not quoted. Yet it shows you God has not asked you to hope for something you can know nothing about. His word does reveal much about heaven.

His Spirit within you will show you heaven is real, as you read the Bible and as you observe the world He has put you in now. Heaven is where Jesus is. Everything in Scripture that points to Him is a glimpse of heaven. Everything in this world that gives testimony to Christ's presence and power, from the gentle butterfly to the giant whale, from the warm sunshine to the softness of the cold snow, from the green grass to the bright stars, from an unselfish act of human compassion to the joy of human love and relationships, from answered prayer to God's daily provision, tells you what eternity will be like.

It is a taste of heaven.

---

[3]If this book has been a blessing to you, or you still have any questions about what the Bible says heaven will be like, the author can be contacted at: DrLarry@eudoramail.com

APPENDIX :

300 QUESTIONS YOU ALWAYS WANTED TO ASK ABOUT HEAVEN

221

ISBN 155369726-X